E243 Inclusive Education: learning from each other

Making it Happen

BOOK 5

This book forms part of The Open University course **E243 Inclusive Education: learning from each other**. The complete list of books and units is as follows:

Book 1 – Starting Out
Course guide
Unit 1   *From here*

Book 2 – Thinking It Through
Unit 2   *The creation of difference*
Unit 3   *Beyond the child*
Unit 4   *The right to have a say*

Book 3 – Listening to Others
Unit 5   *Inclusion in progress*
Unit 6   *Visions, definitions and interpretations*
Unit 7   *Seen but not heard?*
Unit 8   *Professional perspectives*

Book 4 – Working It Out
Unit 9   *Learning to change*
Unit 10   *Changing places*
Unit 11   *Learning from experience*
Unit 12   *At the margins*

Book 5 – Making It Happen
Unit 13   *Inside classrooms*
Unit 14   *A culture for inclusion*
Unit 15   *Agenda for change*
Unit 16   *Imagine better*

Readers

Nind, M., Rix, J., Sheehy, K. and Simmons, K. (eds) (2003) *Inclusive Education: diverse perspectives*, London, David Fulton in association with The Open University (**Reader 1**).

Nind, M., Sheehy, K. and Simmons, K. (eds) (2003) *Inclusive Education: learners and learning contexts*, London, David Fulton in association with The Open University (**Reader 2**).

Making it happen

BOOK 5   Units 13 — 16

The Open University

Education and Language Studies
Level 2

This publication forms part of an Open University course **E243 Inclusive Education: learning from each other**. Details of this and other Open University courses can be obtained from the Course Information and Advice Centre, PO Box 724, The Open University, Milton Keynes MK7 6ZS, United Kingdom: tel. +44 (0)1908 653231, e-mail general-enquiries@open.ac.uk

Alternatively, you may visit the Open University website at http://www.open.ac.uk where you can learn more about the wide range of courses and packs offered at all levels by The Open University.

To purchase a selection of Open University course materials visit the webshop at http://www.ouw.co.uk, or contact Open University Worldwide, Michael Young Building, Walton Hall, Milton Keynes MK7 6AA, United Kingdom for a brochure. tel. +44 (0)1908 858785; fax +44 (0)1908 858787; e-mail ouwenq@open.ac.uk

The Open University
Walton Hall, Milton Keynes
MK7 6AA

First published 2004

Copyright © 2004 The Open University

Edited, designed and typeset by The Open University.

Printed and bound in the United Kingdom by the Alden Group, Oxford.

ISBN 0 749 25308 8

681970B/E243book5i1.1

Contents

Course team

Melanie Nind	*Joint chair and author*
Kieron Sheehy	*Joint chair and author*
Katy Simmons	*Author*
Jonathan Rix	*Author*
Mary Kellett	*Author*
Caroline Roaf	*Author*
Julie Allan	*External assessor*
Brenda Jarvis	*Course manager*
Liz Santucci	*Course secretary*
Alison Goslin	*Designer*
Fiona Carey	*Editor*
Isabel Ford	*Editor*
Chris Gravell	*Editor*
Nicola Tolcher	*Compositor*
Deana Plummer	*Picture researcher*
Demarisse Stanley	*Rights assistant*
Michael Peet	*BBC producer*
Ian Black	*BBC researcher*
Richard Fisher	*BBC Video editor*
Steve Hoy	*BBC Sound dubbing*
John Berry	*Critical reader*
John Swain	*Critical reader*
Sally French	*Critical reader*
Helen Murphy	*Critical reader*
Jim Towers	*Critical reader*
Ronnie Flynn	*Critical reader*

Introduction

Book 5 is the final book of E243. It involves you in discussion of different strategies for making inclusive education happen. These may be at a classroom level (Unit 13), school level (Unit 14) or societal level (Unit 15). They may be part of a prolonged evolution of educational practice or a more radical revolution of systems and practices. We end with a look into the future and engage you in creative thinking about how inclusive education might involve new technologies, new discourses and new ways of teaching and learning.

Book 5 also includes activities related to Video Bands B and A that will help you with your examinable component (interviewing someone whose perspective or role contrasts with yours). The video illustrates the process of interviewing and you are given support to think about the skills and questions involved.

UNIT 13 Inside classrooms

Prepared for the course team by Melanie Nind and Kieron Sheehy

Contents

1 Introduction

In this unit we look inside classrooms at what goes on between teachers and pupils, and between pupils and other pupils. We focus on the detail of day-to-day experiences and explore what makes pupils feel included. Moreover, we discuss what pupils actively do to negotiate their own and their peers' inclusion, as well as how individual staff make a difference. We argue that early years classrooms, with their child-centredness, are particularly ripe contexts for inclusion. Much of what we explore as inclusive practice in these settings, however, can be applied in other settings. We also remind you of the powerful example of inclusive classroom practice in the secondary sector described by Susan Hart in Chapter 18 of Reader 2, which you read in Unit 8.

One of our aims is for you to look more closely at the curricular and pedagogic dimensions of inclusion, and particularly at the interactions between teachers and pupils, and pupils and pupils. We begin by asking whether there is an inclusive pedagogy, that is, a way of teaching and learning that enables the full diversity of pupils to engage with the curriculum. This is partly a question of how teachers think about their challenges and so, as well as looking inside classrooms, we need to look inside minds – an altogether more abstract and less tangible activity! We ask whether inclusive pedagogy involves adopting additional specific methods, effecting a radical overhaul of educational practice, or simply extending the good teaching and learning that already goes on. We apply the social model of disability in looking at how disabling and disadvantaging barriers are addressed or avoided in inclusive classrooms. And we seek models of teaching and learning from which we can learn about the elements that do most to support the active participation of all learners. This leads us, in our third section, to go inside early years classrooms, where diversity and placing the child at the centre of the curriculum are routinely accepted as good practice.

Our fourth section pursues the idea of children and young people, and those who work with them, as gatekeepers of inclusion. We look at what they do to open up or close down opportunities to be part of the action in schools and communities. We want you to reflect on different ways of acting and interacting that are more inclusive and on what works to address or avoid disabling and disadvantaging barriers in inclusive classrooms. In all this we are careful not to forget the policy and resource context, which does not always make a positive contribution to inclusion. This context, nonetheless, is one in which individuals interact and through which they sometimes make inclusion happen. This is the subject of our final section.

Learning outcomes

By the end of this unit you will have:

- gained insights into what might constitute inclusive pedagogy;
- developed an understanding of the kinds of process in which inclusion is actively negotiated;
- reflected on the role of the curriculum in facilitating inclusive education;
- thought about classrooms as enabling or challenging contexts for inclusion.

Resources for this unit

To complete the activities in this unit you need to plan for using the resources as set out in this section. For Activities 13.2, 13.3 and 13.4 you mostly need some thinking time and your learning journal to record your thoughts. For Activity 13.6 you will need to create an opportunity to talk some ideas through with a few friends or colleagues, and in Activity 13.7 you are invited to create a list and pass it on to your peers for sharing.

As part of your study for this unit we will also ask you to read the following chapters:

For Activity 13.1 (and for recapping in Activity 13.4 and 13.8):

- Chapter 19, 'From curriculum access to reflective, reciprocal learning', by Susan Simmons, in Reader 2.

For Activity 13.1 you will also need to have Unit 8 (Book 3) to hand.

For Activity 13.5:

- Chapter 9, 'The Index for Inclusion: personal perspectives from early years educators', by Peter Clough and Cathy Nutbrown, in Reader 2.

During your study you may also wish to complete the following optional readings:

- Chapter 20, 'Gender, "special educational needs" and inclusion', by Shereen Benjamin, in Reader 2;
- Chapter 16, 'Inclusive curricula? Pupils on the margins of special schools', by Melanie Nind and Steve Cochrane, in Reader 2.

2   Is there an inclusive pedagogy?

Traditionally educators have thought about pedagogy – that is, ways of teaching and learning – in terms of two types. These are, firstly, the mainstream pedagogy that goes on in ordinary schools and, secondly, the individualized approaches for particular 'types' of pupils, which are viewed as suited to special school staffing ratios and regimes. The rise to prominence of inclusive education begs the question of whether there is a third type of pedagogy suitable for inclusive education.

The answer to this question, of course, is not straightforward. At the 2000 International Special Education Congress, Richard Rieser and co-presenters spoke of mainstream pedagogy as the elusive quality standard to which pupils sent to special schools are denied access (Rieser, 2000). At the opposite extreme is Gary Hornby and Roger Kidd's (2001) view that inclusion must involve the importing of specialists and specialist techniques into mainstream settings. This is something Mel Ainscow (1997) has argued against quite strongly, maintaining instead that special school practice is incompatible with big, diverse mainstream classrooms, where there are other teaching and learning strengths that can be utilized for the benefit of all.

The idea of the need for different teaching techniques for different categories of 'special educational need' is explored by Brahm Norwich and Ann Lewis (2001), who conclude that there is a lack of evidence to support this viewpoint. If, however, there were special techniques for pupils' different categories of 'special educational need', would there also be special techniques for pupils from minority ethnic backgrounds, for girls, for boys, and so on? Journeying down this road might lead us to conclude that inclusive teaching is individualized teaching and that the teacher's role is to manage a series of individual learning programmes. Perhaps instead this could lead us ultimately to alternatives to learning in classrooms through more radical use of new technologies, which we will explore in Unit 16.

A less extreme example of the individualized teaching scenario is differentiation, in which a common core of learning is made different for different individuals or groups. The thinking behind this is that different pupils may need different ways of accessing the learning, such as more concrete examples, more visual methods, alternatives to ordinary print, or different activities based on their achievements and abilities. Access to the mathematics curriculum for visually impaired students was something sought by Susan Simmons at the start of her action research project, which we will consider in the next activity.

◯ Activity 13.1   More than access

Now read the following chapter:

- Chapter 19, 'From curriculum access to reflective, reciprocal learning', by Susan Simmons, in Reader 2.

As you read highlight or make a note of how Susan Simmons came to understand that inclusion was more than just an issue of access. Why do you think she was able to rethink inclusive education as a more mutual process?

It seems to us that Susan Simmons brought to her research project an openness to ideas and a readiness to learn from others, which enabled her to see alternative interpretations of the 'problem' and solution. Without this she would not have listened to the clear messages the students were giving. She got inside classrooms and talked to people. In this way she engaged with the messy reality of helping to make inclusion happen.

You may find it useful at this stage to think back to Unit 8 and what you learned about the pros and cons of differentiation as a way of responding to diverse learner groups. You may recall that Susan Hart, in 'Learning without limits' (Chapter 18, Reader 2), offered transformability as an alternative: working to *transform* both current patterns of interaction and future possibilities for learning.

Despite reservations we might hold about differentiation and our view that there are some more creative alternatives that are worth exploring, differentiation remains one of the teaching strategies widely understood to promote inclusion. While different people may have different views on what inclusive education is, there is a fair amount of consensus about some of the elements that make up inclusive teaching. These include, alongside differentiation, co-operative learning, peer-mediated instruction, collaborative teaching, classroom management strategies and the teaching of specific social skills (Florian and Rouse, 2001). We explain and discuss these elements in more detail later in this unit, but for now it will be helpful if we think of them as tools in a toolbox, that is, strategies that can be used as and when a teacher finds them appropriate.

In contrast to the toolbox model, we can think of inclusive teaching as being much more of a mind set – a framework for thinking through the decisions to be made in relation to the teaching and learning process. We will turn now to explore what such a mind set or framework for thinking might entail.

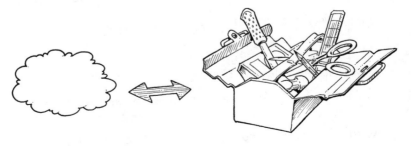

Mind set versus toolbox.

Innovative thinking

Susan Hart is explicit about her view that special language and special techniques are limiting. She explains:

> I have called the book *Beyond Special Needs* because I believe that in order to open up new possibilities we can and should now set aside once and for all the language of 'learning difficulties' and 'special needs'. This language shapes and constrains our thinking, limiting our sense of the scope available to us for positive intervention to a narrowly circumscribed set of possibilities. It has discouraged mainstream teachers from using their knowledge, expertise and experience as fully and powerfully as they might in pursuing concerns about children's learning.

> *(Hart, 1996, p. x)*

For Susan Hart, then, individualizing concerns about children's learning disconnects them from the school processes of which they are a part. Instead, she argues, concerns need to be seen in context, where mainstream teachers are the experts and not special teachers, psychologists or therapists. Hart advocates an approach of innovative thinking which, she explains, is 'not conditional upon the availability of additional support or resources' and which 'does [not] expect teachers to possess superhuman capacities or assume an exhaustive knowledge of literature and research' (1996, p. x):

> What the approach does depend upon is a spirit of open-mindedness and willingness to entertain alternative possibilities. It depends upon the conviction that the picture we currently have of children's characteristics as people, and their abilities as learners, is susceptible to change; indeed, that we have the power and means to bring about changes ourselves by thinking in ways that continually open up new possibilities. I call this 'innovative thinking'.

> *(Hart, 1996, pp. x–xi)*

Hart (1996, p. 102) provides a framework of five questioning 'moves' which help teachers to think in fresh ways about the teaching and learning situation, and to imagine different interpretations from a range of perspectives. The moves involve:

- teachers *making connections* between the learner's responses and the context in which they occur;

- *contradicting*, teasing out and re-evaluating the assumptions underlying our understanding of the situation;

- *taking the child's eye view* to find the meaning and purpose for the learner;

- *noting the impact of feelings* on the situation or our interpretation of it;
- *suspending judgement* while we review our interpretation and resources to act.

This is not a special response to special pupils, but a whole way of thinking. The importance of this kind of mental framework becomes apparent when we see the consequences of teachers questioning their assumptions and beginning to see situations as their learners might see them. One such example is described by Ros Frost (2001) who, while not deliberately using the five moves, suspended judgement on her classroom practice and looked for alternative interpretations for what was going on. The trigger for this was her increasing concern about the behaviour of two boys in her class, Eddy and Todd, and the impact this had on her feelings about herself as an effective teacher. At first she noted the behaviour displayed by the boys on most days, which included attention-seeking noises, not sitting still, talking when others were talking, bad language, damaging others' work and school property, refusal to work and refusal to co-operate or enter the classroom:

> I could feel the pressures begin to mount around and within me. At first I perceived these as challenges, but as the weeks went on I became increasingly worn out from dealing with the unpredictable behaviour of the two children, as well as that of a small handful of others in competition with them ...
>
> Normally I would have coped with these pressures by putting more time and energy into my work. However the physical, emotional and mental demands of managing difficult behaviour now, while needing to maintain thorough planning, assessment and record keeping, had totally depleted these resources ... In retrospect it is easy to see how pressures in these areas built up to such a pitch, yet at the time I was so busy reacting that I was unable to step back and gain a clear perspective on them.
>
> *(Frost, 2001, pp. 17–18)*

After a stressful year in her personal life, these behaviours caused Ros considerable additional stress and she sought the help of the special educational needs co-ordinator (SENCO). Caught in a 'web of professional help' (Thomas and Glenny, 2000), the boys were begun on the official process of registering their special needs and individual behaviour support programmes were devised.

Around this time Ros Frost also began a continuing professional development course which gave her the time and space to interpret her classroom practice differently. She set aside time to observe Eddy, and found that, in a less pressured situation in which she was observing rather than managing him, she could see alternative interpretations for his behaviour, as outlined in Table 13.1.

Table 13.1 Alternative interpretations of Eddy's behaviour

Time	Action	Relaxed interpretation	Stressed interpretation
9.32	Talks when working	Helpful automatic self-expression	Disturbing concentration of others
	Joking	Values friends and humour	Lack of concentration
9.35	Visit friend's table	Needs to relate to others	Disturbing concentration of others
	Asks politely for something	I may have missed this good behaviour from across the room	
	Sharpening pencil	I forgot to organise the helpers	Work avoidance tactic
	'Wooden Willy' action	E's humour; he's happy	Inappropriate behaviour
	Tells friend colour of eyes	Helping his friend	Lack of concentration
9.41	Propels rubber using ruler with description of mechanical catapult	Understanding of technology	Throwing rubber – disruption
	'B' for balloon	Initial sound practice	Disturbing concentration of others
	Birds have stripes	Knowledge of natural world	Disturbing concentration of others
9.45	Discusses friend's eyes and choice of pencil	Accuracy and attention to detail	Disturbing concentration of others
9.46	Stands up and colours at table	Comfortable working position	Disturbing concentration of others
9.50	Describes picture	Expression about relationships	Disturbing concentration of others

(Frost, 2001, p. 21)

Once looking for alternative interpretations, this teacher reflected on whether Eddy's aggression on entering the class was an expression of his frustration partly in response to what she came to see as her inappropriate classroom organization. Further, she 'questioned where the safeguard was for the child against unhelpful teacher behaviour, within the Staged Assessment procedure' (Frost, 2001, p. 18). Her course also enabled her to recognize the wider context, in which she was stressed and overloaded, and the impact this was having on her feelings and practices. Instead of individualizing her responses to the boys, she was able to work on developing herself as the kind of teacher she wanted to be.

This example may prompt all kinds of response in us: we may feel empathy for the teacher's stressful situation or for the pupils' situation; we may be critical of the way Eddy remains a 'case' under professional gaze; or we may ask whether the power balance ever shifted and what Eddy's interpretation of it all was. It does show, though, that when extra resources are called for in inclusion, these resources might very usefully take the form of supported thinking time for teachers and practitioners.

Thinking inclusion.

Interactive pedagogy

The story of Ros Frost's experience is one in which, as the teacher, she came to locate the problem, and the solution, in the context of the school, classroom and curriculum, rather than in the pupil, just as the social model locates the problem outside the person who is disabled. This is not about assigning blame, but about taking responsibility for the context in which difficulties arise, especially when we have some control over what that context is like. This also characterizes interactive approaches in which teaching is constantly evaluated and revised in light of the learners' responses, sometimes on a moment-by-moment basis.

Tony Booth stressed that difficulties in learning arise when there is a mismatch between the learner and the teaching, the task or the materials; 'they indicate a breakdown in the relationship between pupils and curricula' (1992, p. 39). When teachers pitch things badly for pupils, learning is made difficult and a process of exclusion is begun. Conversely, when teachers achieve a good match between learner and learning experience, they enable learners to actively participate in the learning process. Interactive pedagogy seeks to keep the match under review and to achieve the best possible fit between learner and learning experience.

In Chapter 16 of Reader 2, Melanie Nind and Steve Cochrane describe an action research project in which interactive pedagogy was used as part of a drive to promote inclusion. This is an optional reading and you might like to look at it now. The resources used in the project for achieving a good match between teachers and learners can be summed up as:

- the intuitions of practitioners;

- the feedback from learners;

- the input from colleagues as partners in a collaborative process of reflection and problem solving.

Pupils who cause concern are, as we have observed earlier in the course, usually defined in terms of the nature of their 'deficits', as perceived by the education system and professionals within it. Nind and Cochrane, influenced by the social model of disability, regarded them instead as pupils who 'fall outside of the routine competence and confidence of teachers'. This placed the emphasis on enhancing staff competence and confidence rather than on rectifying pupil deficits. This is a more inclusive response than regarding the pupils as belonging in some way under the auspices of a separate kind of teacher and curriculum, that is, in the domain of expert others.

In common with Susan Simmons and with Susan Hart's innovative thinkers, the teachers in Nind and Cochrane's project who had adopted an interactive approach demonstrated a readiness to rethink their approach on the basis of feedback. Thus they turned learning into something that was reciprocal, rather than something than happened to pupils under teachers' control. This happened most successfully when the curriculum framework was based around enabling this to happen, that is, when teachers could work on developing the context that would support the kind of teaching they wanted to enact, based on feedback from their pupils. This is a proactive approach in which teachers see themselves as powerful agents and help pupils to do likewise.

Interacting.

Eve Bearne's study (2002) provides just one example of the kinds of rich feedback children can give on their learning which is 'critical for teachers who want to create inclusive learning environments' (p. 123). You might like to reflect on the children's comments presented below and what they tell their teachers about differentiation and collaboration:

> There are some table settings [of children] that are different so there's stages and the tables are like Canada [who] are on really easy work, India get quite difficult ... and Japan get quite hard work.
>
> *(Year 3 boy, quoted in Bearne, 2002, p. 124)*

> I'm sitting next to Joanne and she helps me if I'm stuck and I help her. Sometimes she helps me know the answer but she doesn't actually like say 'Oh, it's 36' she says 'Well, how many 10s has it got, Leanne, now count the units ...
>
> ... like, when you start she makes you think a lot harder and says 'come on, work it out' because she gives you the first part, like the first number of the answer and then she says 'work it out otherwise I'm not gonna tell you any more' ...
>
> *(Year 3 girl, quoted in Bearne, 2002, p. 123)*

Making connections

So far we have illustrated various ways in which inclusive pedagogy can be understood as an inclusive way of thinking about teaching and learning. Some of our arguments are summed up by Collins *et al.*:

> We need to start from, and value, what our learners bring if we are to avoid a mismatch. We cannot just assume that our learners will adjust to our objectives, priorities and teaching styles. We need to de-centre and see the world through their eyes, so that we can make the curriculum and the learning experience relevant and meaningful.

(Collins et al., 2002, p. 75)

This may be what good teachers have always done and being inclusive teachers may just mean that they have to do it for even more diverse learners. You may recall from earlier units the concept of a 'pedagogy of recognition' (Slee, 1999, p. 200), whereby diverse learners can recognize their own experiences and identities in the curriculum. Julia Preece similarly stresses this need for a local connection: a coalition between the learner's world and the world of teachers and formal education. For her adult education students, who did not readily recognize themselves as learners, the curriculum needed to be culturally or socially relevant. In making the curriculum relevant, 'the trick was to build on people's lived experiences as a knowledge base to construct new ways of seeing the world' (Preece, 2000, p. 10).

Working out from the learner in the way that Preece describes challenges any ideas that 'education is for other people' (Stuart and Thomson, 1995, p. 1). The frequently heard comment among mature students of 'I've never done anything with my life' speaks volumes about perceptions of whose knowledge and reality is seen as important (Stuart and Thomson, 1995, p. 161). Mary Stuart and Alistair Thomson (1995, p. 1) argue that, because 'education [ordinarily] differentiates and limits who can be a learner and what and how she or he can learn', many learners are 'constructed as "other" to the educational norm'. Thus, they have difficulty in engaging with ideas that do not easily connect to, or make sense of, their own particular social experiences. Inclusive pedagogy and curricula challenge this and become characterized by what bell hooks (1994, p. 11) calls 'engaged pedagogy'. This is where 'everyone's presence is acknowledged' and students' lived experiences are not just included but become central to the curriculum, generating the excitement needed for meaningful learning. For us, the tension between this and the national curriculum (or any prescribed curriculum) is marked. As we have seen elsewhere in the course, inclusion presents fundamental challenges to simple transmission models of education in which knowledge is passed down.

▷ # Activity 13.2   Are you connected?

In preparing the teaching and learning materials for E243 we have tried to provide material that allows you to make connections so that you can recognize yourself in the curriculum. Perhaps you are a student who is disabled, or from a minority ethnic background, lesbian or gay, a parent, or working outside the field of education; it was one of our aims to ensure that you should not feel that you have been invisible in our curriculum. Spend a few moments reflecting on times when you felt connected and on ways in which we, as course authors, might have done it better.

Then, if you work in education, think of things you do to work outwards from your learners' everyday experiences. If you don't work in education, imagine yourself in an early years setting, or that you are working on a course like this one. What would you be encouraging your colleagues to think about in order to enhance the inclusive dimension of teaching and learning?

▷ You might have found yourself thinking about the examples and language used at times when you were encouraged to have an emotional response to the course content. You might have thought of particular interactions you have had with your tutor, or interactions that you would want to have with your students or pupils, which communicate that the learner is valued. Judith Watson (2001) writes of the importance of giving learners the opportunity to forge connections, to manipulate information in ways they find personally meaningful, and to work together to negotiate meaning. This involves learners being active, teachers being responsive, and social experiences being integral to and valued in the learning process.

Jenny Corbett (2001) has similarly described inclusive pedagogy as 'connective pedagogy' – a way of working that connects with individual learners and their way of learning, which in turn connects them with the curriculum and wider community. We can think of connective pedagogy as building bridges across our differences.

Jim Sinclair, who has autism, makes a powerful case for this:

> But my personhood is intact. My selfhood is undamaged. I find value and meaning in life, and I have no wish to be cured of being myself. Grant me the dignity of meeting me on my own terms ... Recognise that we are equally alien to each other, that my ways of being are not merely

damaged versions of yours. Question your assumptions.
Define your terms. Work with me to build bridges
between us.

(Sinclair, 1992, quoted in Powell, 2000, p. 11)

Jim Sinclair importantly highlights that the task of making
connections is a reciprocal one that involves all parties. He notes that,
rather than the reality of school and teacher being the normal
reference point against which other realities are judged, difference
belongs equally to both teacher and learner, and in this sense is
mutual. In the reciprocal and mutual process of making connections,
inclusive teachers assume responsibility for questioning their
assumptions and for making the first move to enable the process of
moving towards greater inclusivity to happen. They listen to what
pupils and marginalized groups have to say about their experiences
and use this in questioning their own actions.

Making connections.

Collaborative learning

We have focused on the mental (and emotional) adjustment involved
in inclusive teaching that requires staff to think about their learners,
the learning context and the curriculum in particular ways. We now
look at the way in which collaborative learning can also be seen as
vital to good education and to inclusive education. This does not
mean that there is not a place for the individual learning of some
topics or skills, but that the potential of collaboration is valued and

used. Firstly, we need to understand the characteristics of collaborative learning.

> Collaborating is not just working together towards a common end but also working across differences and boundaries. A simple example illustrates the distinction. A group of learners could cooperate to complete a large-scale picture. This would involve everyone working towards a common end, namely the completion of the picture. Each person might be involved in a number of practical tasks, perhaps preparing materials, drawing the basic design, applying paint and so on. However, if they were simply doing as they were asked this would be co-operation. By comparison, if the views of the participants were sought and their ideas allowed to influence the final outcome then the process would become collaborative. Thus a willingness to collaborate incorporates a readiness for peers to grant and accept authority over each other's work, for example, in terms of peer appraisal. Collaborative learning can also challenge the traditional view of teachers' authority and the way in which that authority is exercised. In this way collaborative learning can be about revitalizing democracy.
>
> *(Collins et al., 2002, pp. 111–12)*

The teacher doesn't have a higher chair.

It is partly because of this overlap between collaborative learning and democracy that collaborative learning is valued in inclusive education. Individuals in collaborative settings are learning the meaning of civic responsibility (Gamson, 1994). Working together, pupils learn to value what others bring to the situation, as they become a resource for the shared project. This of course involves more than working *in* groups, it means working *as* groups.

Collaborative learning, like interactive approaches, can be treated as part of a toolbox of supplementary methods rather than as a whole approach to teaching (Hansen and Stephens, 2000), but this undermines the potential for making a difference. There may be collaborative activity in classrooms but this will be less powerful unless there is also a collaborative ethos or institutional culture of collaboration. Susan Hart describes the 'radically different social climate' of collaborative classrooms in which '*everyone* in the classroom is both a teacher and a learner' (1996, p. 19). Once again, we see the need for a different way of thinking, in which teachers engage with learners in a shared project and give up some of their authority, but not responsibility, in exchange for greater pupil involvement, higher motivation levels, enhanced meaningfulness and richer learning in their classrooms. Collaborative learning involves learning acceptance of different ideas and gives a sense of connection; thus it also reduces isolation and passivity.

The following descriptions of collaborative activity illustrate some of the benefits. In the first example the collaboration of two girls is an unplanned response to a challenge in a design and technology class:

> The girls' immediate response to the requirement for their design to be meaningful was to identify a 'client' for their product. Anna was designing a bath alarm for her grandmother, Nancy a rain detector for a washing line for her mother ... Although the girls were designing different products they had sufficient shared understanding of what a meaningful design meant that they were able to collaborate in the early stages of the project. In their talk at the beginning of the session they brainstormed various interpretations of 'meaningfulness' appropriate to the context of use. Anna suggested designing a package in the shape of a bottle of shampoo for her bath alarm and began to sketch her ideas for the others to consider.

. . . .

Nancy: That looks quite good actually. What about something in the bath? Something to do with water.

Other girl: Yeah.

Nancy: Cause it can go in the sink as well as in the bath. You could do it in the shape of a soap, you could have it in the shape of a sponge, or in the shape of a bubble, the shape of a, no not a tap.

Other girl: A drop thing.

Nancy: Teardrop.

Other girl: A drop of water.

(Murphy, 1999, p. 263)

As Patricia Murphy points out, the girls elaborate on each other's ideas and stimulate each other's thought processes. Even without support from the teacher they reflect together and engage in joint reasoning. Together they work on the problem of how the thing will stand up or be stuck to the bath, thinking strategically for each other in a process that goes on to be reciprocal when they go on to engage with Nancy's design challenge. However, when they become stuck and go to the teacher, he does not voice his thinking aloud as they do, but just offers a solution. The collaboration then breaks down as the shared problem solving around a shared point of reference is gone.

In the next of Patricia Murphy's examples, the collaboration is planned by the teacher but not adequately supported. As in the previous example, the girls' communication styles lead them to articulate their ideas and move into a shared task. It is worth noting that in both examples, while the girls collaborate, the boys work independently and in silence. This illustrates how collaboration is good for learning but also has to be learned and supported as not all pupils are intrinsically drawn to collaborate. Inclusion of all pupils in collaboration often requires planning and support, which can then lead to maximum benefit.

When collaboration is valued by the teacher the pupils understand this, as shown in the final example of purposively selected, mixed-gender groupings.

Rachel: He [the teacher] wants you to listen to other people's ideas and I have started doing that now. Discuss which is the best idea.

Billy: He puts people together he thinks will work, who have the same ideas. Trouble is we get new ideas once we start. He wants us to discuss what we should do, then come up with a final result of what to do.

(Murphy, 1999, p. 267)

Their activity, based on this understanding is collaborative:

> With this much agreed including their common goal, the children went off to collect equipment. They did not allocate tasks, they assumed them and let each other know by talking out loud about what they would do ... The teacher observing the group from across the classroom reacted to the children's activity, i.e. moving from planning to doing, and returned to the group to monitor progress.

. . . .

Teacher: Have you formulated a hypothesis or a prediction of which one will be best?

Seth: Yes, we thought gravel.

The teacher confirmed that this was the view of the other two group members and then left. The children started to carry out their investigation and to monitor each other's decisions.

Rachel: So you are going to start making the holes then?

Billy: Five holes.

Seth: Okay, we want five holes.

Rachel went to get the water. In her absence the boys, who found making the holes difficult, altered the decision.

Seth: [who is making the holes] After a couple of years we should have five holes!

Billy: Why don't we just make it three holes?

Rachel: Returns to group.

Seth: Rachel, we're only having three holes. OK? Because they're big holes.

Rachel: Okay.

. . . .

... The teacher monitored the activity by observing from afar and asking questions periodically. This meant he could keep abreast of the students' thinking and provide appropriate support when necessary. The teacher's questioning technique also placed the decision-making in the children's control. Furthermore, by repeating children's comments he gave them value.

(Murphy, 1999, p. 268)

Murphy goes on to discuss how teachers can use collaborative learning to support boys and girls with their learning strengths and to develop new ways of working. This principle can equally be applied across different aspects of diversity.

Activity 13.3   Collaboration

Try to remember an occasion when you experienced true collaboration with others on something. It might be a project completely unrelated to the course or to education. What was the group trying to achieve together? How might the end product have been different if there had been less collaboration? What was your particular contribution? Did you learn anything about yourself during the process? Make some notes about this in your learning journal and then re-examine them to see if you can make connections between your thoughts and collaborative learning in inclusive education. Next time you engage in a collaborative activity try to pause to reflect on the process as you go along.

For us, as authors, preparing this course has been an extended and intense experience in collaboration. In all likelihood it would have been a very different course without this process and without the contribution of each individual to the whole. Through our collaboration we have learned so much about our own and each other's ideas and styles of writing and working that we are inevitably enthusiastic about it as the only way to work. Our enjoyment of the collaborative process helped us to maintain this approach in the face of other pressures, primarily the fact that it is often quicker, though less satisfactory, to just proceed alone.

Judy Sebba *et al.* (1996) found that staff recognized that working with other adults, particularly support staff, was something they needed to learn. This is a skill now built into the standards for newly qualified teachers in England (TTA, 2002). Teachers working in an open way with other teachers, support staff, pupils, parents and others can achieve so much more than they ever can by working in isolation. Collaborative learning, then, is just as much a part of development towards inclusive education for teachers as it is for pupils.

Strategies for inclusive education

Innovative thinking, interactive and connected pedagogy, and collaborative learning are in some ways philosophies for teaching and learning that are suited to inclusive settings. As inclusive philosophies

Collaborative learning.

they say as much about the power relationships in the classroom as they do about the actual teaching techniques that are used. We now turn to some of the actual tools or strategies that teachers use as part of their inclusive practice. These were elicited by Lani Florian and Martyn Rouse (2001) in their study of inclusive practice in secondary schools, which focused on teachers who have a commitment to inclusive education and are part of a network known as Understanding the Development of Inclusive Schools.

The study looked at the teaching strategies found to be helpful in promoting inclusive practice, which were identified in a review of the literature by Scott *et al.* (1998). These were broadly categorized as differentiation strategies, co-operative learning strategies and classroom management strategies/social skills. More specifically they included things like:

- varying teaching style;
- altering instructions;
- adapting assignments;
- frequent monitoring and feedback;
- peer tutoring;
- offering choice of material;
- teaching self-management skills;
- demonstrating problem-solving strategies.

There were some differences in the strategies used according to the subjects taught; the researchers did not find a pure recipe or formula for an inclusive lesson. Off-the-shelf inclusive lessons are an impossibility because the teaching has to be responsive to the individuals involved, the challenges and opportunities that arise, and, of course, the constraints of the context. For decades teachers have been responding to challenges with strategies of their own design. Sally French (in a personal communication with the authors) recalled a teacher in a further education college in the late 1960s giving up all blackboard work so that Sally, with her visual impairment, would not be disadvantaged. This strategy itself is less significant than the willingness to seek out a solution and adopt it. While practitioners can become more skilled in specific strategies, it is likely to be their inclusive outlook, philosophy or way of thinking that ensures that they seek such strategies and make them work in their situation. We explore this idea further in Unit 14.

A useful distinction between traditional and inclusive practice is offered below. This illustrates how the reference points, resources and way of approaching the challenge of learner diversity are quite different in inclusive or 'inclusionary' practice.

Activity 13.4   Mapping the terrain

Table 13.2 below presents an analysis contrasting the features of a traditional approach and an inclusionary approach.

Consider the distinctions made and, as you do so, think back to Susan Simmons's chapter, which you read in Activity 13.1 (Chapter 19, Reader 2), and reflect on the examples of inclusive teaching and learning that have appealed to you in this and other units. How do these examples map on to the dimensions of the inclusionary approach on the right? Are there links with any dimensions on the left? How useful are the distinctions that are made?

Table 13.2   A comparison of traditional and inclusionary approaches

Traditional approach (which may include integration)	Inclusionary approach
Focus on student	Focus on classroom
Assessment of student by specialist	Examine teaching/learning factors
Diagnostic/prescriptive outcomes	Collaborative problem solving

Student programme	Strategies for teachers
Placement in appropriate programme	Adaptive and supportive regular classroom environment
Needs of 'special' students	Rights of all students
Changing/remedying the subject	Changing the school
Benefits to the student with special needs of being integrated	Benefits to all students of including all
Professionals, specialist expertise and formal support	Informal support and the expertise of mainstream teachers
Technical interventions (special teaching, therapy)	Good teaching for all

(Porter, adapted by Thomas et al., 1998, pp. 13–14)

We found a good match with the features of the inclusionary approach on the right and few links with the traditional items on the left. The possible exception might be 'focus on student', since much of the inclusive practice, while not focusing on the students' deficits, does focus on the students' prior knowledge, interests, learning styles and emotions. Nonetheless, it remains true that the practitioners and writers we have drawn on focus their attention on classroom interaction and school practice. It is just that the teacher seeks to work with and learn from the whole pupil rather than dwell on 'needs'.

3 Inside early years classrooms

Some of you may have found the discussion so far a little too abstract for your taste. One of the problems with making this less abstract is that this is relatively new ground in education and research. Much more is written about inclusive policy than inclusive practice. More attention has been given to why inclusion is important than to how it is enacted. Case studies of schools like Bangabhandu can help to bring inclusive practice to life, but their staff would be the first to admit that they have much more work to do yet in experimenting with what works in terms of inclusive teaching and learning.

From the child out

One way to gain a better understanding of what life is like inside inclusive classrooms is to look at early years classrooms where there is often an acceptance of the principle of inclusion and readiness to enact this. This is perhaps because early years classrooms are furthest removed from exclusionary pressures, or because resistance to these pressures is strong. Chris Lloyd is not unusual in arguing that 'the principles which inform early years education can be seen to provide for the whole of education a model of genuine inclusion' (1997, p. 172). She explains the principles of early childhood education further:

> They begin with the learning processes of the child, recognising different rates of development and making allowance, therefore, for the widest range of abilities. Indeed, as the starting point is what the child can do rather than what she or he cannot do, there are inevitably more possibilities to include a wider range of difference and diversity from the onset. The view of adults as enablers, responsible for structuring and managing a challenging and stimulating learning environment which emphasizes opportunities for creativity and play, as well as a rich variety of personal interactions, is also compatible with an inclusive view of education. There are opportunities within this approach for capitalising on difference and diversity and for laying emphasis on a very wide range of possible abilities and skills.
>
> *(Lloyd, 1997, p. 177)*

If, as Chris Lloyd argues, inclusive education is based on a human rights model, this means planning and conceiving the whole educational provision from a different perspective. It means moving on from ideas of difference as a deficit to be corrected, to recognizing and valuing a broader and more diverse spectrum of what is considered normal or ordinary. It is this greater tendency to value diversity and to keep a diversity of children together that characterizes the early years phase of education, even though disabled children may often be segregated later. Early childhood educators have emphasized valuing who children are here and now, as three year olds for example, rather than as four or five year olds in the making. This is a principle of early years education and is conducive to inclusive thinking. We might think of the challenge as being one of how to retain this ethos in later phases of education, when formalized curricula and assessment frameworks tend to work against it.

◯ Activity 13.5   Inclusion by numbers?

Now read the following chapter:

- Chapter 9, 'The Index for Inclusion: personal perspectives from early years educators', by Peter Clough and Cathy Nutbrown, in Reader 2.

As you read the chapter, identify what additional reasons the authors offer for early years classrooms being models of inclusive education.

You may have identified the issues of positive attitudes towards diversity in early years education settings and also how early years teachers see themselves. The description of the reception teacher's response to a child with developmental delay illustrates this:

She was reassured by the head that it was not a scenario of 'success or failure' and was given support to evaluate her own practice in a way which led her to believe that her established skills of providing a well structured and stimulating learning environment for all children were particularly relevant for Steven. She realised that it was her duty to attend not only to what was 'special' about Steven, but also to what was 'ordinary' and that there was no mystique to analysing tasks. She was already doing this and making them accessible to all children, including children with learning difficulties.

(Herbert, 1998, p. 103, cited in Reader 2, p. 86)

Similarly, the perspectives of the early years educators show their concern that the ordinary nursery should be the first option, or the norm, for all children, and therefore the need to get it right from the start – to begin as one would wish to continue, that is, inclusively. Hannah Mortimer also gives a good example of inclusive thinking when she asserts that 'Early years educators do not have to be experts in special education in order to meet these needs; they are, already, specialists in how young children learn and develop' (1995, p. 165). There may be all kinds of ways in which children with sensory impairments or autism, for example, might learn differently, but with an inclusive mind set these are seen in the context of the qualities all children have in common.

There is considerable consensus amongst early years educators about what constitutes an appropriate curriculum framework for the early years (Owens, 1997). For children under three this is the activities and experiences provided by educators; the activities devised by the children themselves; all the language and communication they are involved with and which is around them; and all their sensory stimuli (Rouse and Griffin, 1992). The key issues are seen as children's need for relationships with significant responsive adults and their need for nurturing and developmentally appropriate learning experiences. The curriculum should be seen in terms of processes rather than content, and of interlinked areas of development that are planned holistically, all of which make use of the social context and play environment. This approach places emphasis on the quality of how children learn and on helping them become good learners, as opposed to any subject-type knowledge they might acquire.

A mismatch is beginning to creep into early years work between the expectations of the national or formal curriculum and a developmentally appropriate curriculum centred on the child. Since the institution of the national curriculum, teachers of pupils with severe learning difficulties have had to grapple with a similar mismatch. They have been caught between joining in because the national curriculum is for everyone and questioning whether it is helpful for anyone. They have grappled with a range of tensions including:

- previous notions of good curricular practice versus the national curriculum;

- balance and breadth on one hand, and differentiation and relevance on the other;

- entitlement to access – but access to what?

With a strong desire to be inclusive, these teachers have often opted to use national curriculum subjects as contexts for working on personally relevant work alongside others following formal curriculum work. Using frameworks like the one described by Nind and Cochrane (Chapter 16, in Reader 2), in which subject-related processes, general processes and learning-to-learn processes are kept in balance, allows a curriculum which is inclusive for pupils who are young or developmentally young. Thus, a lesson might be planned to support pupils working on the science processes of testing, observing and comparing; the general processes of listening, watching and waiting; and the learning-to-learn processes of attending, exploring and anticipating.

Activity 13.6 Act your age?

One of the complex issues that arises from this discussion is how much of what goes on in classrooms does and should look radically different for learners of different ages. We have already noted the need to build on the learner's own world, which is well accepted in early childhood education and in adult education. But what about for learners between the ages of five and nineteen? How much should the content of learning be dictated by a person's age? What about the way in which they learn? Should the willingness of teachers to be inclusive be different at different schooling levels?

Try to gather the views of a few friends or colleagues on this issue. Do their ideas spark off different thoughts for you?

Completing this activity is a good rehearsal for the final ECA.

We have always found this to be a lively topic for debate. What is appropriate as practice for learners of different ages tends to be something people hold strong views on. Notions tend to be internalized as common sense, so it is easy to lose sight of the ways in which our ideas about behaviours for particular age groups are cultural and constructed, rather than natural. It raises issues about respect, but also sometimes highlights intolerance of people whose abilities and behaviours are not matched with expectations for their chronological age. This is not something that can be side-stepped in inclusive education and our own view is that age-related norms can act as a straightjacket and militate against an ethos of valuing diversity. For example, having to fit in with other 12 year olds and do what other 12 year olds do can be a real tension for pupils during their transition into secondary school.

Focus on the learning environment

The way in which many early years classrooms are inclusive classrooms can be illustrated by the way in which early years practitioners think about responding to pupils who cause them concern. Melanie Nind, one of the course authors, was asked to help facilitate an action research project when a mainstream early years department found they had a number of pupils with limited communication and language abilities. With their inclusive orientation, the early years educators did not want to adopt the deficit model of identifying the specific needs of the individuals concerned and developing individual programmes for them. Instead, what suited their context was an inclusionary framework as outlined in Table 13.2 above.

Moreover, the practitioners concerned recognized that communication and, equally importantly, communication learning and communication difficulties do not just involve the child. They also involve the child's communication partners – the adults and children they interact with on a daily basis. This was a communication issue for pupils *and* staff, and in response to this the focus of research became the communication environment and the verbal and interaction behaviour of the adults, rather than on individual problems in the children (Nind, 2003).

The participants in the study began a cycle of observation, discussion, action and reflection. This led to efforts to make verbal interactions less adult-dominated and more child-led, less directive and more responsive. Thus, in the inclusive, collaborative approach to solving the 'problem' the team worked to make the learning environment more effective, without labelling or segregating individual children.

The team wanted to understand and do more of the activities that support rich communication and language, and one spontaneous end of the afternoon session became a focus for discussion. The children came to the front and reported on what they had been doing that afternoon and the immediacy of the subject matter helped to make conversation flow. They then chose who was to have a turn next and this power over the classroom dynamic was highly motivating. The following extracts from the transcript show how the teacher resisted dominating the talk and how, when given the power to do so, the children successfully involved each other.

. . . .

John:	I been outside playing with Toby and Matthew. What was it again we were playing with, them things, the window cleaners?
Teacher:	Mmm, are you going to choose someone to swop with?
John:	No, I ain't finished. I was with a boy and with Colin and Steve and when it was tidy up time I quickly got that time thing.

Teacher:	Was that the sand timer?
John:	Yeah, were we quick yeah?
Teacher:	Mmm. Have you finished telling your news?
John:	Yeah. I choose Buddy.
Buddy:	I been playing with ... (lists half a dozen names) (Pauses – hands go up from children wanting next turn, shakes head at several children, exaggerated facial expression to show difficulty in choosing.) Vincent.
Teacher:	So many to choose from. Okay Vincent, tell them your news.
Vincent:	I was sticking. I choose, er, Geoff.
Teacher:	Thank you Vincent.
[...]	
Harry:	I been ... Geoff is talking. I been doing making a fire engine. A big one. Build and build and then Darren had a good idea. Put two wheels like (pause) like (pause) and attach them like.
Teacher:	That was a big word you used then, attach. I bet if I asked them they wouldn't know what that means.
Harry:	What does attach mean? (*hands go up*) Darren
Darren:	It means get lost.
Harry:	No. Sid
Sid:	It means put together.

(Nind, 2003)

. . . .

Jane Danielewicz *et al.* (1996) studied children's discourse patterns and power relations in one teacher's sharing time as it evolved from a teacher-led to a child-led format. In the action research project, the team wanted the children to enjoy similar benefits gained from enhancing the group's participation. The four year olds in this session, like those in Danielewicz *et al.*'s study (1996), used language for social relationships and achieved greater participation and more collaborative dialogue than the teacher often did. They rehearsed getting and holding the floor, telling stories, playing with language and hearing each other's perspectives, and the talk and learning were meaningful.

An observation of a later session illustrated more ways in which this kind of early years classroom activity facilitates inclusion, as the field-notes illustrate:

> The children's things brought in from home for showing have already been gathered. The children are seated on the carpet and the teacher's chair is vacant – Caroline is

on the floor with the children. There is an atmosphere of anticipation that makes the children bubbly so establishing quiet before they begin takes a little while. Caroline [teacher] chooses Benjamin to begin because of how helpful he has been – this is a privilege. She reminds them of the rules, when someone is speaking they must listen carefully, the person on the chair talking can choose two people to ask questions and is responsible for selecting the next person for the hand over of roles.

Benjamin's language is rushed and not easy to follow, but he is enjoying leading.

...

There is genuine shared interest here.

...

The next child in the chair is more animated and has a stronger idea of how to tell a story – but they are interested in the toy – the focus is on the things not the language – *is this a good or bad thing? Will lively language come out of the interest in the toys?*

...

H is concerned with the rules, slightly stressed about negotiations. K is clearly much more confident with language. She knows its power, combined with her lively performance, to hold an audience.

...

Caroline asks one of the Turkish children to ask another Turkish child if she likes the toy 'Fizz'. There is a quick exchange in their home language and he reports back, "she said yes", the girl is smiling broadly. I am moved by this – the way peers are used to support each other – the way the girl is brought into the activity. *Now I wonder – Can this grow into questions with more than single word answers?*

...

Confusion here with grammar, she doesn't use 'she', it isn't corrected, I think Caroline's right to leave it – this isn't the time or place. Caroline has kept a very low profile – her talk has not dominated at all – but now she is anxious about the time and so is intervening to move things along – this is the teacher's need to use language to manage that we have talked about.

(Nind, 2003)

These excerpts also show how teachers in early years settings are able to share power with the children and enable their active involvement, and how the children can in turn enable the active involvement of each other.

Activity 13.7   What works in inclusive education?

In their report of a study of what works in inclusive education Judy Sebba and Darshan Sachdev (1997) summarize some of their findings as follows:

- Classroom teaching is at the heart of developing inclusive education.
- Developing inclusive education requires teaching strategies that enable all pupils to participate and learn for as much of the time as possible.
- Pupil participation and learning can be enhanced by high expectation, drawing on pupils' previous experiences and maximizing peer support.
- Variety of teaching methods is regarded by pupils as a critical factor in learning.

(Sebba and Sachdev, 1997, p. 46)

Based on what you have read so far, and any relevant experiences of your own, think about how you might modify or develop this list. You might like to send your list to your tutor, peers or course team so that together we build a bigger list.

4   Pupils as gatekeepers of inclusion

Different discourses, different roles

It is not just young children who play a role in inclusion. Julie Allan's (1999) study showed how children in primary and secondary schools act as gatekeepers of inclusion. Her in-depth study of the everyday experiences of a group of pupils in mainstream education in Scotland, some of whom were disabled, showed that pupils' behaviour towards each other oscillated. The way their behaviour wavered was linked to how their ways of thinking wavered – between medical, charity and rights models. Mostly pupils guided and supported the inclusion of their peers with 'special educational needs'. But they also sanctioned some exclusion as part of regulating and normalizing their experiences; it was okay to be different only within certain parameters.

Pupils operated according to their ideas of their peers as deserving or undeserving of their support, which in turn was linked to ideas of fairness. The discourse of deserving, for example, was: 'they [people with Down syndrome] are humans, so should be treated the same as us' (Allan, 1999, p. 32). This contrasted with the undeserving discourse of, for example: there is 'nothing wrong with her ... just too lazy and doesn't feel like doing the work' (p. 33). Similarly, pupils 'with special educational needs' were evaluated in terms of 'like us/ not like us' (p. 34), as 'mainstream' pupils grappled with how to respond to difference. The following excerpt of dialogue illustrates how operating this mental framework in relation to Susan, a wheelchair user, was not straightforward for them:

. . . .

G   I'd say treat her just like us.

J   Yes, but try and help her as well.

JA   Yeah?

G   Help her as well, yeah but treat her like us, no offence or anything.

JA   What do you mean by no offence?

G   Well, I don't want to make her feel left out or anything. I think she should just join in whatever she can. The same as we do.

J   But try and help if she needs help, but try and treat her like us as well.

G   Yeah.

(Allan, 1999, p. 34)

. . . .

The pupils Julie Allan observed and talked to adopted different roles. The pastoral role involved protection of peers and concern for their well-being. For example, they would walk Phillip, who had a physical impairment, home from school. There was also a punitive role and, importantly for this unit, a pedagogic role as pupils took responsibility for academic as well as social experiences. Pupils described some of their pedagogic strategies:

'You've got to keep asking him or he'll never know.'

'If he writes something down wrong, we'll tell him to do
the right thing, or we'll tell him how to spell something.
Unless we don't know how to spell it.'

(Allan, 1999, pp. 35–6)

Julie Allan discusses how pupils were not passive in the processes in
which inclusion was negotiated, but rather active agents in the
process of inclusion/exclusion. They often challenged or crossed
boundaries imposed on them by others. They chose to make more or
less of their impairments and to help to shape how others viewed
them. They saw themselves as active in working towards achieving
their desires rather than in 'meeting their needs'.

Negotiation within parameters

When we go inside schools and classrooms, then, we see that inclusion
does not just happen to pupils; they have a part in actively
negotiating it. You may like to complete the optional reading,
Chapter 20 in Reader 2, at this point. In this chapter, Shereen
Benjamin reminds us that there are constraints on how pupils can
enact their lives. Gender expectations, for example, have a significant
impact on the options open to pupils as they seek to establish their
identities and friendships in school. She cites one boy's mother who, in
interview, sums up the situation for him:

> He obviously wasn't a clever boy, not in the usual sense of
> the word, and the boys were either clever or good at
> football, it had to be one or the other, and poor Ryan,
> well, he just didn't fit in. There was another child in his
> class, she was a sweet little thing, Ryan used to like her,
> they sat on the same table, and they both went to [the
> Learning Support Unit] together, and she used to play
> with the little infants at playtime, but Ryan could hardly
> do that, could he, a boy his size?

(Interview, Greyhound School, quoted in Reader 2, p. 251)

Negotiating inclusion for Ryan is not just about his learning or co-
ordination difficulties. It involves the implications of these, combined
with being a boy in a situation where there are certain expectations of
what boys can and should do. In contrast, another boy in another
school is able to transcend gender expectations:

> Ken tells the children to get into groups of four. There is
> instant noise and movement, as children negotiate their
> groupings. I zoom in on Stephen, who remains sitting,
> cross-legged, looking up and around him with a look of
> utter bewilderment on his face. I am somewhat surprised
> when Jermaine goes over to him, invites him to stand up,
> then puts an arm around Stephen's shoulder and
> negotiates for them both to join two girls. I wouldn't have
> been surprised if one of the high-status boys, or a girl, had

looked after Stephen in this way. But I would have
thought that Jermaine, who always seems to have an
insecure grip on both academic and micro-cultural
success, and who often acts 'macho', would have been
resistant to grouping himself with a boy with SEN and
two girls.

(Fieldnotes, quoted in Reader 2, p. 257)

Perhaps Jermaine has more options because in this inclusive school
climate there has been a 'freeing up [of] room for manoeuvre by both
girls and boys' (Reader 2, p. 257). As Benjamin proposes, ' "help" is
recast as shared pursuit of success, boys can take up helping and
helped roles without consequent loss of masculine status, and girls
who are struggling can access help without needing to position
themselves as overly vulnerable or ultra-childlike' (p. 257).

In researching inclusive classrooms, the authors, together with other
colleagues, have analysed a lot of the everyday interactions between
pupils at George Holt Community Primary School (Benjamin *et al.*,
2003; Hall *et al.*, 2002). In Ken's year 6 classroom of 11 year olds,
where we focused our attention, there were many examples of peers
supporting each other. Like the pupils in Julie Allan's study, they took
on pedagogic roles in helping to take responsibility for each other's
behaviour and learning. On one occasion Ken was out of the
classroom dealing with pupils in crisis and the rest of the class were
left to get on. Various pupils took on the role of supporting Leanna, a
pupil who often struggled, and two girls looked across at her work and
praised her for her neat writing. On another occasion Ken was
imparting a lecture about the importance of the children not wasting
their talent and while he was in full flow Leanna arrived late and, not
being able to find a vacant chair, crouched down near her place
without causing disturbance. When he came to a stop Ken gave
Leanna a marble (part of an intricate reward system) for coming in
quietly. One pupil started to clap and others joined in communal
celebration of Leanna's achievement.

The pupils at George Holt whom we observed facilitating the
participation of others did so in a school culture that supported this.
The school had buddy and lunchtime patrol systems, whereby pupils
were trained to organize playground games, spot and befriend lonely
children and sort out minor conflicts. They were expected to be
independent in resolving everyday classroom problems. The teaching
incorporated paired-reading activities and frequent collaborative
learning.

The lessons learned through an era of integration have taught us that
placing a child in a mainstream context does not necessarily mean
that she or he is included. Inclusion means being part of the school
community, and enjoying the ties and connections we have with
others that give us a sense of belonging and that help our emotional

well-being (Cole and Lloyd, 2002). This sense of community is achieved when we recognize that we can achieve so much more together than we ever could alone. A lesson learned from poorer countries, where peer support is readily used (Ainscow, 1999; Mittler, 2000), is the value of collaboration. Here, as everywhere, inclusive pedagogy means mobilizing the resources of teacher–teacher, teacher–pupil and pupil–pupil support for inclusive ends.

5 Inclusive practice against the odds

Mixed messages

In this final section we pause to focus on the context beyond the classroom to reflect on how this influences what goes on within classrooms. We acknowledge the various forces against inclusion that people in schools have to cope with. Barriers to inclusion in the classroom are to some extent determined by economics and the wider exclusion of certain devalued groups in society. The course has presented the arguments for inclusive education and cited national and local policy initiatives that have followed the international, human rights led drive towards inclusion. But it would be misleading if we did not recognize that the policy context is mixed and confused, with forces for and against inclusion. The inclusive practice going on inside classrooms that we have described is developing in spite, as much as because of, the policy context.

The backdrop is an educational marketplace in which schools are driven by agendas of financial survival as much as educational values. In England the pressures imposed by national testing and league tables mean that schools strive to meet artificial targets and benchmarks, at the same time as they seek to ensure the meaningful participation and achievement of all. The pressures from outside and above have led many into setting, streaming and whole-class teaching. Inclusive practice flies in the face of many of these pressures and represents a strong position adopted by the individuals involved.

The whole standards agenda and routine national testing (Standard Assessment Tasks or SATs) constructs some children as failing, or in the Department for Education and Employment (DfEE) (1999) terms as not reaching the expected standard for their age. The contrast could not be greater than with the inclusive education agenda, which exhorts schools to reduce barriers to learning (Benjamin, 2002). For some schools and teachers the standards agenda drives everything they do and how they think about it. For others, in contrast, an inclusive agenda is dominant. There are other options, though, as Florian and Rouse (2001) explain:

Schools in England face dilemmas about how they should respond to two conflicting demands from government. The first demand is for higher academic standards and the second is the call for the inclusion of children with special educational needs in mainstream schools. For some schools these demands are incompatible, but for others, policies and practices that support inclusion are emerging as the means by which they may be able to raise academic standards for all children.

(Florian and Rouse, 2001, p. 399)

We must remember that pupils may be high or low achievers, regardless of some disabilities or differences, but Florian and Rouse's argument here is that teaching diverse groups makes teachers better practitioners. This was borne out in evidence gathered concerning the positive effect on standards of inclusive secondary education in Newham:

One secondary comprehensive has a signing cohort of deaf pupils and about six per cent of pupils have a statement for learning or emotional difficulties. The headteacher reported that A–C grade passes at GCSE had doubled since the inclusion policy had begun. Some staff believed that inclusive teaching (as opposed to coping with one-off placements) had increased their expertise in differentiating the curriculum during this period to the benefit of all their pupils. During observations it was noticeable that signing had become another language in the school used by staff and hearing pupils ...

(Alderson and Goodey quoted in Sebba and Sachdev, 1997, p. 26)

This connects with Mel Ainscow's (1999) argument that if teachers adopt a 'transformative' rather than 'normative' orientation, then pupils who are difficult to teach become a stimulus for helping them to question and enhance their practice. You may be able to recall this happening in Julie's practice, in Susan Hart's chapter 'Learning without limits' (in Reader 2). Engaging with difference in this constructive and reflective way is not, however, what is encouraged by the Government documentation on standards for teachers. The Standards for England and Wales, for example, require teachers to 'recognise and respond effectively to equal opportunities issues as they arise in the classroom' (TTA, 2002, p. 58, S3.3.14). Similarly, the Scottish Standard for Full Registration indicates that teachers must 'value and promote fairness and justice, and adopt anti-discrimination practices in all regards, including ... disability' (GTC Scotland, 2002, p. 24). The problem with these statements is that they construct difference as problematic; they push the new teacher towards the management of, rather than engagement with, difference. Early years educators have often united to resist unwelcome pressures or imposition of practice. As we saw earlier in this unit, they have often shared a clear sense of best practice in the early years, which includes child-centredness and not the national or any other formalized curriculum. Geva Blenkin and Vic Kelly are clear about the problems of the downward pressure from the type of curriculum imposed on older children:

> a curriculum divided into subjects is, potentially, the most alienating form of curriculum for young children because it formalizes experience too soon and, in doing so, makes it distant from the everyday, common-sense knowledge and learning that the young child is familiar with and responsive to.

> *(Blenkin and Kelly, 1993, p. 58)*

Blenkin goes as far as to describe a 'head-on clash' (1994, p.37) between the national curriculum and the traditional early years curriculum, with the former being the 'mirror image' of the latter, 'its exact opposite in every respect' (p. 40).

In early years, and beyond, there have been real fears that an over-emphasis on narrow core skills leads to neglect of emotional and other kinds of learning which are left to chance (David, 1998). This is inappropriate for an inclusive curriculum, which should be inclusive of and value the full spectrum of skills and abilities – the whole person.

Sadly, drives from central government have often steered schools towards an individualistic ethos, 'dominated by individual work programmes with the message of "do your own work and don't interfere with others"' (Collins *et al.*, 2002, p. 114). Individualized, competitive teaching approaches have received greater official endorsement than the collaborative, inclusive approaches we are concerned with. Teachers who have resisted the appeal of such endorsement have understood that such approaches encourage pupils to become teacher-dependent, passive and poorly motivated, rather than able to draw on their own resources and those of their peers in a learning project which they are committed to.

Moments of inclusion

Some pupils go to schools where there is an inclusive ethos. Such schools may be in the process of considerable change as the cultural shift towards inclusion is carried forward, as you will find in the next unit. For others the school, like the wider context, may be much less supportive of inclusive values and practices, but pupils may still enjoy moments of inclusion (Benjamin *et al.*, 2003). This is a concept very different from the all or nothing view of inclusion. Moments of inclusion may be negotiated by individual staff and pupils supported by, or in spite of, the context. When we were filming at Bangabhandu School, we noted a teacher, while going about the task of monitoring the children's group work, getting a coughing child a glass of water. In this moment she communicated an empathy with the child and her value of him. In another London school we observed a teacher giving constructive criticism of the children's work carefully sandwiched between praise for their efforts, two children recording their stories on tape rather than on paper, and a pupil offering a loner in the playground the chance to join in with him and his friends. These moments of inclusion happened against a backdrop of schools and government professing strong inclusion polices but sending out mixed messages about their seriousness about them.

The moments of inclusion we have described are worth recognizing because our power as individuals to change everything we dislike in education may be limited, but our potential to make a difference remains significant. Moments of inclusion can paradoxically be experienced frequently and felt quite strongly in special schools and the challenge becomes one of bringing these experiences to other contexts. The idea of individual resilience and individual power to make a difference has emerged elsewhere in the course. In terms of teaching and learning there are two prime ways in which individual staff can make moments of inclusion happen. One is through the emotional connections they might make and the other is through the decisions they might take.

Feeling included means feeling connected, valued and cared for. bell hooks (1994) recalls this feeling at her local Black school in the racially divided American South, where the teachers 'made sure they knew us ... our parents, our economic status, where we worshipped, what our homes were like, and how we were treated in the family' (hooks, 1994, p. 3). She compares this with the emotional void in the big, mixed school where no one took the time to know her. The lesbian and gay teenagers who spoke to Colm Crowley described not being able to be themselves at school and 'switching off' (Chapter 15, in Reader 2, p. 180) or even opting out in order to survive. In contrast, the study club for lesbian and gay youth offered not just a supportive environment but a learning culture in which the students could be themselves and direct their own learning. Similarly, Janet Collins (in Chapter 17, in Reader 2) illustrates how pupils who, for a range of reasons, don't connect and don't become actively involved in the curriculum pay a huge price in terms of their poor learning and their negative views of themselves as learners. She argues that schools need to reach out into the real lives of pupils to build connections.

At George Holt Community Primary School, Ken made decisions that made a difference to his pupils. He chose to teach them strategies so that they could support each other in paired reading and he gave his pupils the option to work in ways that suited their different styles. When he was teaching from the front of the class he used examples based on the children's street knowledge, drawing them in and enabling them to make connections. Support staff reflecting on their roles (see for example Chapter 19 by Caroline Roaf in Reader 1) are aware that their work involves them in a series of on-the-spot decisions, the consequences of which may mean that a pupil is included or excluded. In turn, how teachers decide to utilize the human resource of a learning support assistant can facilitate or detract from pupils' social and academic involvement in the class.

▷ Activity 13.8   Making different choices

Susan Simmons's chapter, which you read for Activity 13.1, contains many examples of decisions made by staff and others that had positive or often negative consequences for the students' inclusion (Chapter 19, in Reader 2). Skim through the chapter again and identify some of the more negative ones. Then imagine yourself in the role of teacher/learning support assistant/ head of department/media resources officer, whichever role is appropriate for the examples you have found, and think about what decision or action you might have taken to create moments of inclusion rather than exclusion. As you do this think about the influences on our decision-making in such circumstances.

Simmons communicates much of her sense of frustration when bad choices were made and important organizational decisions were out of her control. Looking at this from a distance, we can see how the schools sometimes lacked the all-important inclusive school culture or ethos that might have led individuals towards different choices. Individuals were often working under pressure and were unable to take time to reflect, opting instead for what seemed pragmatic at the time. Using Susan Hart's innovative thinking framework or the *Index for Inclusion* (Booth *et al.*, 2000) might have empowered the individuals involved to operate a more inclusive agenda.

6 Conclusion

In this unit we have addressed the pedagogic and curricular dimensions of inclusive education. We have asked what goes on inside inclusive classrooms. Our exploration has identified some specific strategies that teachers adopt, but more importantly it has illustrated the particular mind sets that inclusive teachers have that influence the decisions they make and actions they take. Some pupils with particular impairments will need or choose to learn in particular ways. Specialist teaching (such as Braille techniques or mobility training for blind children) cannot be forgotten. But inclusive education necessitates that these specialist elements are delivered sensitively and in context, and do not frame the whole educational experience of the child.

Our discussions have steered us towards recognition of the common ground occupied by good practice and inclusive practice. There is a danger here that we might lose some of the clarity around what makes something inclusive as opposed to good. But there is the bonus that we come to understand inclusive practice not as something special and distinct, once again something only special teachers can do, but as characterized by the best of good teaching and learning being extended to all. Much of the practice we have celebrated as inclusive is not new; the fact that much inclusive practice has been going on for decades demonstrates how do-able it is. Fostering this further involves teachers working together to learn from each other and, just as importantly, to learn from the people they teach – looking for, recognizing and responding to feedback.

Building a picture of inclusive pedagogy.

References

Ainscow, M. (1997) 'Towards inclusive schooling', *British Journal of Special Education*, **24**, pp. 3–6.

Ainscow, M. (1999) *Understanding and Development of Inclusive Schools*, London, Falmer.

Allan, J. (1999) *Actively Seeking Inclusion: pupils with special needs in mainstream schools*, London, Falmer.

Bearne, E. (2002) 'A good listening to: year 3 pupils talk about learning', *Support for Learning*, **17**(3), pp. 122–7.

Benjamin, S. (2002) *The Micropolitics of Inclusive Education: an ethnography*, Buckingham, Open University Press.

Benjamin, S., Nind, M., Collins, J., Hall, K. and Sheehy, K. (2003) 'Moments of inclusion and exclusion: pupils negotiating classroom contexts', *British Journal of Sociology of Education*, **24**(5), pp. 547–58.

Blenkin, G. M. (1994) 'Early learning and a developmentally appropriate curriculum: some lessons from research' in Blenkin, G. M. and Kelly, A. V. (eds) *The National Curriculum and Early Learning: an evaluation*, London, Paul Chapman.

Blenkin, G. M. and Kelly, V. (1993) 'Never mind the quality: feel the breadth and balance' in Campbell, R. J. (ed.) *Breadth and Balance in the Primary Curriculum*, London, Falmer.

Booth, T. (1992) E242 *Learning for All*, Unit 1/2, *Making Connections*, Milton Keynes, The Open University.

Booth, T., Ainscow, M., Black-Hawkins, K., Vaughan, M. and Shaw, L. (2000) *Index for Inclusion: developing learning and participation in schools*, Bristol, CSIE.

Cole, A. and Lloyd, A. (2002) 'It's not what you know it's who!: enabling and supporting community involvement' in Carnaby, S. (ed.) *Learning Disability Today*, Brighton, Pavilion in association with the Foundation for People with Learning Disabilities/Tizard Centre.

Collins, J., Harkin, J. and Nind, M. (2002) *Manifesto for Learning*, London, Continuum.

Corbett, J. (2001) 'Teaching approaches which support inclusive education: a connective pedagogy', *British Journal of Special Education*, **28**(2), pp. 55–9.

Danielewicz, J. M., Rogers, D. L., and Noblit, G. W. (1996) 'Children's discourse patterns and power relations in teacher-led and child-led sharing time', *International Journal of Qualitative Studies in Education*, **9**(3), pp. 311–32.

David, T. (1998) 'Learning properly? Young children and desirable outcomes', *Early Years*, **18**(2), pp. 61–5.

Department for Education and Employment (DfEE) (1999) *National Learning Targets for England 2002*, Sudbury, DfEE.

Florian, L. and Rouse, M. (2001) 'Inclusive practice in English secondary schools: lesson learned', *Cambridge Journal of Education*, **31**(3), pp. 399–412.

Frost, R. (2001) 'Children and teachers with special needs' in Dadds, M. and Hart, S. (eds) *Doing Practitioner Research Differently*, London, RoutledgeFalmer.

Gamson, Z. F. (1994) 'Collaborative learning comes of age', *Change*, **26**(5), pp. 44–50.

General Teaching Council (GTC) Scotland (2002) *Scottish Standard for Full Registration* [online], Edinburgh, GTC. Available from http://www.gtcs.org.uk/gtcs/menu_link.aspx?MenuItemID=274&ID=71&selection=7 [accessed 17 November 2003].

Hall, K., Collins, J., Benjamin, S., Sheehy, K. and Nind, M. (2002) 'Assessment and inclusion/exclusion: the power of SATs', BERA Annual Conference, University of Exeter, 12–14 September 2002.

Hansen, E. J. and Stephens, J. A. (2000) 'The ethics of learner-centred education', *Change*, **33**(5), pp. 40–8.

Hart, S. (1996) *Beyond Special Needs*, London, Paul Chapman.

Herbert, E. (1998) 'Included from the start? Managing early years settings for all' in Clough, P. (ed.) *Managing Inclusive Education: from policy to experience*, London, Paul Chapman.

hooks, b. (1994) *Teaching to Transgress*, London, Routledge.

Hornby, G. and Kidd, R. (2001) 'Transfer from special to mainstream – ten years later', *British Journal of Special Education*, **28**(1), pp. 10–17.

Lloyd, C. (1997) 'Inclusive education for children with special educational needs in the early years' in Wolfendale, S. (ed.) *Meeting Special Needs in the Early Years: directions in policy and practice*, London, David Fulton.

Mittler, P. (2000) *Working Towards Inclusive Education: social contexts*, London, David Fulton.

Mortimer, H. (1995) 'Welcoming young children with special needs into mainstream education', *Support for Learning*, **10**(4), pp. 164–9.

Murphy, P. (1999) *Learners, Learning and Assessment*, London, Paul Chapman.

Nind, M. (2003) 'Enhancing the communication learning environment of an early years unit through action research', *Educational Action Research*, **11**(3), pp. 347–64.

Norwich, B. and Lewis, A. (2001) 'Mapping a pedagogy for special educational needs', *British Educational Research Journal*, **27**(3), pp. 313–29.

Owens, P. (1997) (ed.) *Early Childhood Education and Care*, London, Trentham.

Powell, S. (2000) 'Learning about life asocially: the autistic perspective on education', in Powell, S. (ed.) *Helping Children with Autism to Learn*, London, David Fulton.

Preece, J. (2000) 'Challenging the discourses of inclusion and exclusion with off limits curricula', Working Papers of the Global Colloquium on Supporting Lifelong Learning [online], Milton Keynes, Open University. Available from http://www.open.ac/lifelong-learning [accessed 28 September 2000].

Rieser, R. (2000) 'Inclusion: a human rights issue, voice of the oppressed', International Special Education Congress, Manchester, July 2000.

Rouse, D. and Griffin, S. (1992) 'Quality for the under threes' in Pugh, G. (ed.) Contemporary Issues in the Early Years, London, Paul Chapman.

Scott, B. J., Vitale, M. R. and Marsten, W. G. (1998) 'Implementing instructional adaptations for students with disabilities in inclusive classrooms: a literature review', Remedial and Special Education, 19(2), pp. 106–19.

Sebba, J., Ainscow, M. and Lakin, S. (1996) Developing Inclusive Education at Rawthorpe High School: report of the first phase of the evaluation, Barkingside, Barnardos.

Sebba, J. and Sachdev, D. (1997) What Works in Inclusive Education, Barkingside, Barnardos.

Slee, R. (1999) 'Policies and practices? Inclusive education and its effects on schooling' in Daniels, H. and Garner, P. (eds) Inclusive Education, London, Kogan Page.

Stuart, M. and Thomson, A. (1995) (eds) Engaging with Difference: the 'other' in adult education, Leicester, National Organization for Learning.

Thomas, G. and Glenny, G. (2000) 'Emotional and behavioural difficulties: bogus needs in a false category', Discourse: Studies in the Cultural Politics of Education, 21(3), pp. 283–98.

Thomas, G., Walker, D. and Webb, J. (1998) The Making of the Inclusive School, London, Routledge.

Teacher Training Agency (TTA) (2002) Qualifying to Teach: handbook of guidance, Summer 2003. Available from: http://www.tta.gov.uk/assets/training/qtsstandards/handbook_of_guidance.pdf [accessed 17 November 2003].

Watson, J. (2001) 'Social constructivism in the classroom', Support for Learning, 16(3), pp. 140–7.

UNIT 14   A culture for inclusion

Prepared for the course team by Jonathan Rix and Katy Simmons

Contents

1 Introduction

In this unit we will consider some of the reasons why inclusion is difficult to achieve. We will explore the degree to which people have to want to achieve inclusion for it to become a reality, and how generating such a desire across our schools and communities is requiring us to develop new cultures of learning and organization. To explore these ideas effectively we will expand on some of the ways in which we can come to understand the cultures of schools and the ways in which they change.

It is important to remind ourselves that despite the resistance that inclusion commonly faces there is much that is encouraging for us to draw upon. We will consider some recent strands of research into school improvement, school effectiveness and inclusion and touch upon some of the conflicting ideas that these put forward. We will also touch upon how the notion of inclusion is kept in the forefront of our minds and highlight the importance of keeping up the pressure if we wish to produce an inclusive education system.

We will then go on to discuss the factors that have been identified as fundamental to producing cultural change and outline some of the practical means that will generate that cultural change within schools. By the end of the unit we hope you will have an understanding of how inclusive education requires a cultural shift in the ways many of us work and think within education, but that such a cultural shift can be realistically (and enjoyably) achieved.

This unit aims:

- to consider the nature of school cultures and their impact on inclusion;
- to examine how people can start to change a school culture.

Learning outcomes

By the end of this unit you will:

- have an understanding of the ways of describing a school's culture;
- have considered constraints upon change and have an appreciation of how change can be brought about;
- be able to critically appraise the degree to which a school culture is ready to change and in what ways it may need to change;
- be able to relate the material in this unit to the video material in Unit 5, reflecting on how you perceive the roles of managers and policies in relation to changing school cultures.

These learning outcomes will be assessed in the TMAs.

Resources for this unit

For Activity 14.6, you will need to read:

- Reader 1, Chapter 24, 'Unequivocal acceptance – lessons for education from the Stephen Lawrence Inquiry' by Robin Richardson.

For Activity 14.8, you should watch:

- Video Band A, 'Interview with Helen Jenner'.

2 What stands in the way of inclusive practice?

Throughout this course we have highlighted the tensions that exist between different policies at local and national levels. In Unit 13 we considered some of the factors that can hinder the creation of inclusive practice. We noted the impact of the marketplace and parental choice, national testing, league tables, target-setting and the widespread standards agenda. We considered how these influences have encouraged a return to the use of setting and streaming, increasing the constraining impact of formalized curricula such as the national curriculum. These factors are all immensely powerful forces working against the principles of inclusion, but they are by no means the only forces at work.

The reforms that occurred during the 1980s and 1990s were presented as opportunities to empower head teachers and governing bodies, but in many ways schools were merely being empowered to do the Government's bidding (Wallace and Pocklington, 2002). As governments attempted to implement their policies through a process of encouragement, regimentation and assessment, a state of almost perpetual reform was created, in which schools were having to respond to ever more complex external initiatives. The impact of such change upon the working and personal lives of teachers and head teachers, was, and is, considerable. That impact is also felt by students, their parents and their communities. No wonder it often arouses great hostility!

Teacher attitudes

It is against this backdrop of constant change and institutional and individual stress that the development of inclusive schools is taking place. The response of teachers will be fundamental as to whether these inclusive policies work (Forlin, Douglas and Hattie, 1996), but many teachers already feel shell-shocked at the amount of change they are having to undergo. As one learning support assistant (LSA) says in Caroline Roaf's chapter in Reader 1, 'It's almost as if their [teachers'] job is becoming wider but you are setting much, much higher targets for them to achieve' (Reader 1, p. 225).

Teacher unions have sometimes responded by taking positions that act as barriers to inclusion. The Suffolk County Division of the National Union of Teachers, for example, circulated advice to schools in 2002 entitled 'Saying No to the inclusion of pupils with a history of violence'. This advice included checklists for risk assessment and possible additional resourcing requirments, and then a means of calculating whether admitting the child into the school will be in breach of the provisions of the Health and Safety At Work Act. This reflects rising concern among teachers about dealing with violent and antisocial behaviour, such behaviour being often linked with behavioural, emotional and social difficulties (BESD).

Most research into the attitudes of mainstream teachers towards both integration and inclusion of children with special educational needs also offers little support for change. Generally speaking, teachers say they are in favour of inclusion in principle but doubt its practicability (Croll and Moses, 2000). Thomas Scruggs and Margo Mastropieri (1996) examined research into teachers' attitudes towards inclusion/integration over 37 years in 28 studies and found that while two-thirds of the teachers supported the notion of inclusion, less than half believed it was a realistic option for most children. Only one-third felt that mainstream was the best setting for disabled people to learn in, and less than one-third believed they had the resources, time, skills or training to include people with special educational needs. Interestingly, these figures remained roughly stable over the years. In addition, the more severe teachers perceived students' needs to be, the less they supported inclusion.

Local government attitudes

Change has taken place at all levels of the education system. Local education authorities (LEAs) have undergone as much as the schools and teachers within them. These changes have taken place at both a macro and a micro level. LEAs' interventionist role, and their powers and responsibilities, have been weakened. In 2000, their responsibilities, were defined as:

- special educational needs;
- access and school transport;
- school improvement and tackling failure;
- educating excluded pupils and pupil welfare;
- strategic management.

(DfEE, 2000, p. 8)

These functions were those that central government did not believe could be delegated to schools. Although LEAs' strategic role remains significant (as does their power within statutory assessments), they have argued that the reduction in the funding they can retain has had a major effect on their ability to proactively intervene and assist in supporting individuals or in the support regime a school offers.

Set against this loss of control there is also evidence that some LEAs' negative response to inclusion can damage the inclusive process within schools and across the authority. For example, LEA officers have been shown to have contradictory definitions of what inclusion means, commonly viewing it as integration by a different name (Ainscow *et al.*, 1999). They are also identified as 'pretending to adopt' government policy while carrying out what they think is the 'most appropriate' set of actions for local conditions (Ainscow and Howes, 2001). So, while government documents such as *The Distribution of Resources to Support Inclusion* (DfES, 2002) provide exemplars of good practice and encouragement to LEAs who have not yet adopted them, there is no enforcement mechanism for those LEAs who choose to ignore the need for change.

Parental and pupil attitudes

One of the groups who have supposedly gained power in place of LEAs is parents. This is a diverse group, of course, whose views will change across time and often depending on the provision their children are receiving. Nonetheless, we can see that the group often finds itself caught between different theoretical camps. Parents can be uncertain about the merits of inclusion, receiving mixed opinion from 'experts', while only wanting the 'best' for their children. They want the best social environment, the best academic environment, the best personal environment, the best cultural environment and the best physical environment. There are bound to be contradictions.

These contradictions are highlighted in particular when parents compare mainstream and special school placements. Campaigns to maintain funding for special schools, such as that run by the Barbara Priestman School, Sunderland, often focus upon these contradictions:

> Barbara Priestman School is a special school dedicated to meeting the individual and special needs of some very special children. Life is never going to be very easy for them. For many of them inclusion in mainstream schools will be no answer and bullying will be a threat. They have a variety of physical disabilities or some learning difficulty. These make it a bit more difficult for them to access the national curriculum and lead straightforward lives.
>
> Some are delicate, others have sensory impairment. Many have quite complex needs that advocates of inclusion may not know about and certainly may not understand.
>
> *(Barbara Priestman School, 2003)*

The Barbara Priestman campaign was aimed at stopping Sunderland LEA from closing the school down. It was long-running and well organized. It gained many signatories for its campaign, and lobbied David Blunkett, then Secretary of State for Education and Employment. The campaign articulated the concerns of the school and parents who did not share their LEA's inclusion agenda and who saw it as, at some levels, a simple excuse to reduce the provision made for their children.

Pupils, too, find themselves caught up in the confusion about what will be 'best' for them. As is made clear in Joy Jarvis *et al.*'s chapter in Reader 1, pupils' views can seem as contradictory as their parents' (Reader 1, Chapter 18). In many ways they demonstrate the most extreme examples of conflicting behaviour. Anastasia Vlachou, for example, reports that children say they will not play with a particular child because of a sense of 'difference', but then proceed to do so. She notes the demand for a 'high degree of conformity', but she sets this against the culture that creates those notions of difference and normalcy:

> Inclusion ... touches on the formation of self, and the ideologies and values to be found in wider societal culture. Nowhere was this reflected more than in the discussions I had with the children. Discussions with children can reveal important messages about the nature of society in which we live. It is through these discussions that one can realize that what are predominantly viewed as natural and neutral occurrences are in fact socially created ideologies, history congealed into habit.
>
> *(Vlachou, 1997, p. 168)*

Activity 14.1   Reflecting on childhood

Consider some ways in which socially dominant attitudes in your childhood affected how you behaved. What do you think of that behaviour from your current perspective? Consider also what it was that gave different young people power among your peers as a child. To what degree were adults aware of or involved in these relationships?

One of us remembers a popular activity from the playground (mid-1960s) as being shooting German soldiers (not 'Nazis'). This demonstrated a cultural obsession with guns and the Second World War, and a widely accepted xenophobia.

One of us remembers teasing another pupil because he cried when the whole class was caned (mid-1960s), and another remembers being in awe of the peer who had the new Clash album (mid-1970s). In the first instance the pupils were copying their teacher's mockery; in the second pupils felt that no adult could know anything of the significance of the Clash.

Where does this leave us?

A major factor in all the barriers outlined above is the response of individuals to the notion and reality of inclusion and how it affects their ways of doing things. It boils down to whether individuals really believe in it or not.

The importance of people's commitment to the ideas behind change is not peculiar to the notion of inclusion. It is reflected in our traditional responses to any change and development. Consider the model in Figure 14.1 (from Wallace and Pocklington, 2002). Contained within this model are all the negative factors and responses mentioned above, as well as the positive factors which are our goal.

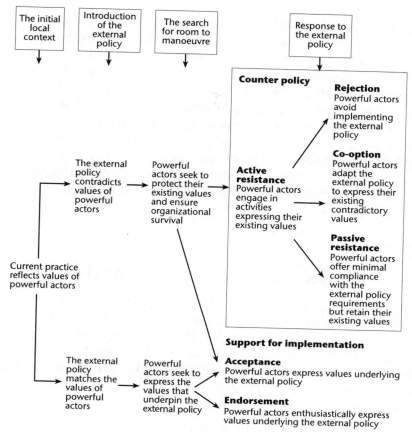

Figure 14.1   How organizations respond to change (from Wallace and Pocklington, 2002, p. 67).

▷ ## Activity 14.2   Reactions to change

With a friend or colleague, discuss changes that they have recently experienced in any organizational setting. It could be a workplace or community setting; it could be a family activity or a change in management structure. Explore with them their attitudes to the changes and how their attitudes compared with others in that setting. See if you can identify responses outlined in Figure 14.1.

This will help prepare you for the ECA (examinable component assignment).

When we consider our responses to changes in our past we may or may not feel proud of our actions. Dealing with change may mean coping with feelings of loyalty that we have to ourselves and to others and to the systems in which we operate. Prioritizing loyalties is always difficult. We also have to decide how far we are willing to sacrifice time and energy for the things we are loyal to. It is easy to make mistakes. It is easy to misplace loyalty. Once we have invested time and energy in an idea, we tend to believe in it and don't want to give it up. This is the barrier that needs to be overcome in those who see inclusion as a threat. We have to encourage everyone to be willing to question their beliefs and practices, because achieving the implementation of inclusive practice requires wholehearted support for the values that underpin it (Corbett, 2001; Zollers *et al.*, 1999; Vlachou, 1997).

3 Understanding cultures and change

So how do we gain the support of powerful 'actors' so that inclusive policies express their values and are thus accepted and endorsed at all levels of the education system? To achieve this requires a change in the culture that creates and supports the values which they express. We need therefore to consider in slightly greater depth the nature of organizational cultures. Edgar Schein (1984) offered a formal definition:

> Organizational culture is the pattern of basic assumptions that a given group has invented, discovered, or developed in learning to cope with its problems of external adaptation and internal integration, and that have worked well enough to be considered valid, and, therefore, to be taught to new members as the correct way to perceive, think, and feel in relation to those problems.
>
> *(Schein, 1984, p. 2)*

'The way we've always done things' is perhaps a simpler way to describe this idea of organizational culture, but either way culture remains something that is largely intangible. How do we pin down the basic assumptions? We touched on this in Unit 5, introducing Schein's ideas regarding three levels that reveal the culture: artefacts, values and underlying assumptions. Another useful descriptive tool is Gerry Johnson's 'cultural web'. Johnson (1992) suggests the following ways of observing the culture in action:

- Routines – typical behaviour towards each other and those outside;
- Rituals – formal and informal occasions that emphasize special events;
- Stories – formal and informal narratives that describe people and events, success and failure;

- Symbols – physical, social and cultural labels (titles, language used, items in the environment) that reflect status within and ideas about the organization;
- Power structures – formal and informal structures based on rank, knowledge, or skills;
- Control systems – assessment and reward systems, emphasizing what is important to the organization;
- Organization structure – formal and informal structures that delineate relationships and processes.

Activity 14.3   Analysing an organization

Consider an organization you know well and try to think of an example of each of the descriptors in Johnson's web. You might think of the local playgroup, for example, and the way in which the children are greeted on arrival each day, how special days are celebrated, families referred to and so on. Or you might consider your own workplace and how the hierarchies of management are apparent in its symbols and daily rituals.

Then try to imagine what sorts of examples you would expect to be able to come up with for an inclusive educational setting.

One of us talked about the daily morning meeting within a secondary school they know. The potential for this routine meeting to become an important ritual is undermined by the accepted practice of staff wandering in late. This is a failure in the power structure, a failure underlined by management's constant reminders to staff at the meeting about the importance of being at the meeting on time. The process has become a story that is regularly brought up with a sigh and shake of the head (particularly in the smoking room).

We decided that in an inclusive setting people would want to be at the meeting on time because they'd feel they were missing something and that the organization was missing something if they weren't there.

Inclusion, improvement and effectiveness – a clash of cultures?

Terrence Deal and Allan Kennedy link ideas of cultural change with ideas of bereavement: 'Cultural change typically creates significant individual and collective loss' (Deal, 1985, p. 294). Hardly surprisingly, this means that there is a strong reaction towards change. Michael Fullan (1991) describes the consequences of this reaction as the 'implementation dip'. After the new idea is generated, it needs to be implemented and then become part of everyday practice. The dip occurs because of the destabilization and uncertainty that is caused by the change being put into place.

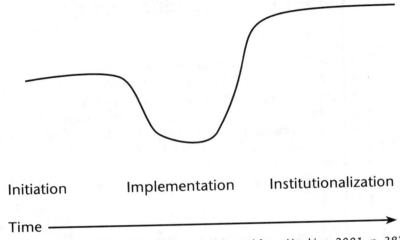

Initiation   Implementation   Institutionalization

Time

Figure 14.2   Fullan's implementation dip (adapted from Hopkins, 2001, p. 38).

Our genuine emotional and intellectual attachment to what we know, and the threat this poses to effective change, means that the ways we go about changing organizational culture must be both justified and effective. If we are to change systems so as to bring about lasting inclusive practice, then that must generate an improvement in schools and their effectiveness, or many will readily reject the changes as inappropriate. As Richard Elmore has noted, 'studies of curriculum reform repeatedly find that new ideas fail to take root in the practice of teachers because those ideas are not reinforced in the immediate work environment of students and teachers' (Elmore, 1995, p. 365).

During the last few years the research base of school effectiveness and the methods of school improvement have become much more closely linked (Hopkins, 2001). But at the same time they have been seen as in some ways in conflict with the development of policy and research in the field of inclusion (Slee and Weiner, 2001; Florian and Rouse, 2001). Lani Florian and Martyn Rouse (2001) point out that researchers in inclusion and special educational needs have tended to question the methodological, ideological or political stance of much school effectiveness work, since it fails to appreciate the context of diversity in which many schools operate. Mel Ainscow (1999) considers that theories of school effectiveness and school improvement have a tendency to produce checklists of successful components or strategies. In contrast, in carrying out his own research into school improvement he has found that the complexity of the challenges presented belies the existence of any such 'quick-fix' solutions. He suggests that evidence from these fields of research makes them suitable starting points in the 'process of internal review'. This approach fits neatly with the notion of inclusive practice as an ongoing process.

Mel Ainscow and David Hopkins were two among many involved in the school improvement project, Improving the Quality of Education for All (IQEA). Both of them have independently identified six similar conditions that need to be in place for school development to occur:

- a commitment to *staff development*
- practical efforts to *involve* staff, students and the community in school policies and decisions
- 'transformational' *leadership* approaches [which distribute power and encourage ownership]
- effective *co-ordination* strategies
- serious attention to the potential benefits of *enquiry and reflection*
- a commitment to *collaborative planning* activity

(Hopkins, 2001, p. 96)

On considering these conditions it is easy to see how espousing such values is relatively easy, but that effectively applying them requires a genuine commitment, and therefore a culture that will transform the ideas into underlying assumptions about how to deal with the day-to-day.

Keeping up the inclusive pressure

The cultural change associated with our vision of inclusive education will not create itself. Many schools and schooling systems will only adopt new ways because of the pressure upon them to do so. This does not mean the change need be unsuccessful, just so long as genuine cultural change underpins developments.

Pressure for change comes from a wide variety of sources. In Unit 15 we will consider the role that individuals and pressure groups can play in driving change, but it is worth drawing attention to some drivers of change in this unit too.

First, it is important to bear in mind broad legislative and policy changes, the latter transmitted through Government documents such as guidelines and codes of practice, as well as Government sponsorship of documents such as the *Index for Inclusion*. Schools are increasingly expected to consider cultural change within their own situation. The fact that Government sends such material to mainstream schools affects the awareness and therefore the thinking of teachers and administrators. This in turn stands a chance of permeating through to processes and practices.

Secondly, we must take into account the work of campaigning organizations which gather and distribute information, such as the Alliance for Inclusion, Parents for Inclusion (PI), the Refugee Council and the Institute of Race Relations. Such groups are not just trying to change the culture within schools and government, but also the underlying assumptions of people in the wider community. If every school has an inclusive culture it will largely be meaningless if the students and parents who use the school do not share or understand the beliefs that underpin it.

Witnessing cultural change

There is plenty of evidence of genuine cultural change that has occurred during the last few years. In Unit 5 we discussed the changes within Newham and Tower Hamlets. Similarly, at the time of writing there appear to have been some changes in the underlying culture of the London borough of Lambeth. Local parents, disabled adults and disabled young people in Lambeth were brought together by PI to share a vision for the future and to consider the obstacles and problems that get in the way of that vision. Based on this research, PI then launched a report for service-providers in Lambeth and in 2002 began to run workshops for statutory and voluntary organizations.

An Early Years inclusion officer has been appointed by the LEA, and out of the Early Years Development Childhood Partnership have come inclusive policies and action for all of Lambeth's early years provision. Jo Cameron of PI told one of the authors in 2003 that she felt the changes in the borough were very much coming from the grassroots. A lot of this was due to disability equality training, which was 'opening eyes and minds of schools' and because 'more and more people are enabled to challenge the status quo'.

Lambeth has demonstrated the struggles that LEAs face. Alongside moves to develop an inclusive culture, some people wished to merely reinvent the old model. There was a vocal group wedded to the ideas of special schools and this group was listened to by local councillors and officers. Though the numbers of students being educated in special schools had decreased, the borough was still planning to spend £10 million on the facilities of two special schools to make them 'centres of excellence'. At the same time they were building three primary schools and one secondary school that were physically accessible to all and which would themselves become centres of excellence for different 'special needs'; when we were writing this, we did not know whether students would be in mainstream classes. Lambeth was therefore offering three models of education: segregation in special schools, partial segregation in attached units, and inclusion in the early years.

Clearly, changing a culture is complex and requires long-term commitment to win the hearts and minds of those involved. One particular problem is that institutions and systems can contain a multitude of cultures (Kilmann *et al.*, 1985) so that it is not a matter of altering just one set of underlying assumptions. There is evidence within schools that change can be effective, however. In the US the Comer School Development Program generated improvements in a whole range of areas, though not in attempting to develop inclusive practices in particular:

> Many observers ... have found that students improve in a whole range of areas – self efficacy, relationships with peers and adults, general mental health, achievement on standardized tests, and classroom grades. They also have fewer suspensions, less deviant behavior, and better attendance. In addition, the researchers found that teachers, too, have better attendance, that both students and parents rate the school climate more highly, and that parents participate more frequently in school activities ...
>
> It requires deep cultural changes in the school and district ... Simply designing and placing a shared decision-making structure in a school setting is unlikely to be effective unless there are supportive components.
>
> *(Squires and Kranyik, 1996, pp. 29–30)*

Unfortunately, there is still a lack of empirical research into schools attempting to become inclusive, but the signs are that school cultures and those working within them can change positively across time, despite pockets of resistance. Clarke *et al.* (1999) attempted to evaluate four comprehensive schools developing 'in this more inclusive direction', and found that there was still a level of resistance to the ideas and practicality of the approach in schools that had spent more than a decade moving in this direction.

Alan Dyson and colleagues carried out research into eight primary and secondary schools and found they varied in their success in becoming more inclusive, but that 'given the right combination of circumstances and commitment, individual schools may be fundamentally changed' (Dyson *et al.*, 2002, p. 10). Alison Bishop and Phyllis Jones (2002) studied the response of 90 students in initial teacher training to a series of workshops involving individuals from special schools and their specialist support staff. Despite a high level of nervousness at the outset of these sessions, the students' responses were overwhelmingly positive and led to a greater self-confidence about their own abilities.

4 What produces successful change?

In this section we will consider four factors that have been identified as important for successful change.

Wanting to change

As we touched upon earlier, the most fundamental requirement is a real desire for change. Dyson *et al.* (2002) noted that the schools that most successfully developed new inclusive practices were those which were already questioning their systems and ways of working. These schools had 'found it necessary to try alternative solutions to the problems of disengagement in their pupil populations' (Dyson *et al.*, 2002, p. 8). This desire for change must come from every part of the organization. If people are developing inclusive practice merely in response to top–down policy change, they may not embrace the values and so not 'wrestle with and solve the difficult issues that arise from school wide changes in curriculum, staffing, assessment, and instructional practices' (Zollers *et al.*, 1999, p. 164).

As Skrtic and Sailor (1996) point out, if individuals are excluded or alienated, then the 'democratic community' is threatened. People need to be involved because, firstly, it is their right, and, secondly, if they have a sense of ownership then they are more likely to be enthusiastic about the change. If they do not have a sense of ownership they will tend to do only enough to cope with the change without actually embracing the process and ideas behind it. As Kilmann *et al.* (1985) propose, top–down changes may be easy to initiate but are difficult to maintain and are likely to produce visible compliance rather than genuine acceptance. Participative approaches are more difficult and time intensive, but tend to produce wider, more lasting change to which people are publicly and privately committed.

People, particularly teachers (Brighouse and Woods, 1999), like to be autonomous in many aspects of their lives, but school-wide policies can still generate a desire in staff to be involved and to generate effective change. Waterhouse (2002) talks about two schools in Scotland (Stevenson High School and Scott High School) that responded to a 1998 Government-sponsored initiative to reduce the exclusion of pupils. Both schools appointed behaviour support teachers who worked solely on behaviour support and were available at all times to assist in disruptive situations. This member of staff could work with students and staff to explore new ways of working. Both schools wished to intervene early in situations, and to move from a coercive and punitive culture to a supportive one. Members of the senior management team became more visible during the day and bureaucratic ways of dealing with both staff and pupils were reduced. Problems with pupils 'were now dealt with holistically by a whole-school team'(Waterhouse, 2002, p. 14). In both schools exclusions dramatically reduced in one year, from 118 to 26 in one school and from 80 to 56 in the other.

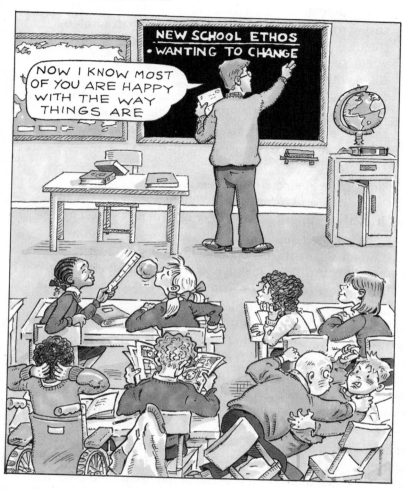

Leadership

Zollers *et al.* (1999) examined the culture of one school that was attempting to be inclusive. They noted that implementing inclusive practices can generate feelings of vulnerability as practices and structures are reconstructed. They also identified three underlying characteristics to counterbalance this and encourage successful change, namely the importance of the leader, a broad vision of the school community, and shared language and values.

The importance of leadership is an essential ingredient in successful change to inclusive values (Cole, 2003). This leadership needs to go beyond defining a direction and gathering support. It needs to become 'sophisticated and differentiated' to move ideas beyond simply being a vision (Wallace and Pocklington, 2002). A commonly suggested approach is called transformational leadership:

Transformational leadership encourages followers to reach beyond their self-interest to embrace some group goal advocated by leaders. It embodies:

idealized influence – leaders are charismatic, acting as strong role-models for followers who wish to emulate them, expressing high standards of ethical conduct which win followers' trust and respect and provide them with a sense of purpose

inspirational motivation – leaders communicate high expectations, engaging followers in developing and making a commitment to achieving a shared vision whose compass extends beyond their immediate concerns

intellectual stimulation – leaders encourage followers to be creative and innovative, to challenge their own and leader's assumptions, and to engage in problem solving

individualized consideration – leaders create a supportive climate where they encourage followers to identify their diverse individual needs, facilitate their efforts to meet these needs and so promote their development.

(Wallace and Pocklington, 2002, p. 214)

The head teacher (principal) in the study by Zollers *et al.* (1999) clearly demonstrated a transformational style of leadership. He 'facilitated open discussions and resolved conflicts collaboratively' (p. 164), and in so doing inspired, encouraged and supported the members of the school. In his particular case, he also acted as a strong role model, demonstrating that a 'significant visual impairment' need not be a disability.

It can be seen that one of the main achievements of the transformational leadership approach is that it allows the followers to take an active role in decision making in regard to their own actions and the actions of others. This spreads the notion of leadership more widely. We are all able to become leaders in different ways and at different times. We are all encouraged to take ownership of situations and issues. In the video you watched during Unit 9, Jimmy Kane, a founder of Penn Green, talks about the need for a vision, linked to social justice and good citizenship, shared by a critical mass of staff who can keep the vision going through hard times.

Within schools, therefore, notions of leadership should not concern only the head teacher and senior management but must be spread throughout the school (Ainscow, 1995 and 1999). This goes beyond delegation of authority. Visser *et al.* (2002) highlight a need for a 'critical mass of staff' who are committed to the values of inclusion. This critical mass varied in size but needed to include 'key players'. When we consider who the 'key players' within a school might be, however, we may well be in for a surprise. A very chatty member of the kitchen staff may have considerably more influence over people than a rather grumpy Head of English.

Activity 14.4   Leadership

Consider the ways in which you have carried out formal and informal leadership roles at different levels within social groups. How significant have these different leadership roles been in affecting the behaviour and practices of different social groups?

These roles might include organizing a training session, collecting money for an absent colleague, or helping someone who is lost within the building.

Community

When we begin to expand our ideas of leadership at every point within the system we can also begin to reconstruct our ideas of a school community. Zollers and colleagues expand this notion to 'allow all members of the school and the neighbourhood to join the school community' (Zollers *et al.*, 1998, p. 168). In effect this resulted in concerted efforts to bring parents into the day-to-day life of the school and more closely involve them in the education of the children. This is a very limited notion of 'all members', however. Community schools in Scotland, as we saw in the Bannockburn video and discussed in Unit 9, are positioning themselves as educational centres for everyone's learning, not just young people and their families. This model is enormously variable too. Meldrum Academy in Aberdeenshire, for example, has a police station and the public library included in it. The original plans for comprehensive education in England and Wales was for this community model too.

The notion of community behind these ideas of schooling can also be questioned. Are we referring to all the people who live around the school, or those who are involved in the school, or perhaps within a community of faith? Ian Martin describes how communities grow out of the shared experiences of individuals. Our personal experiences will always separate us from others to a certain degree but some of our experiences will be shared by enough other people for us to gather around them. They will not usually be common enough, however, to be shared by all people. Here lie the voices of minority groups who are marginalized by the majority. Their community is created out of the experience of being excluded from the mainstream. This creates definite challenges for the development of inclusive practice:

> Notions of the inclusive community have their limits precisely because such communities (plural) are often formed in response to their exclusion from the wider community (singular).
>
> *(Martin, 2000, p. 3)*

 ## Activity 14.5   Excluded communities

. . . .

Think back across this course. Consider all the different communities that we have discussed who have their identity reinforced through 'exclusion from the wider community'. Now that you have reconsidered the communities more commonly recognized as being excluded, interview a friend or colleague about the different excluded communities in which they have been involved. Ask, for example, how these communities were excluded, and how did they come to recognize that others shared their experiences?

This will help prepare you for the ECA.

· ·

Our education system is constructed around a very narrow norm of behaviour and expectation, yet within this system we wish to include all those who are used to being excluded from aspects of the culture that created that norm. If we wish to overcome this separation by creating an inclusive school that reflects the community in which it exists that school must therefore be a reflection of both the pluralistic and singular notions of that community.

Crow and Allen (1994) identify four key points that help us to work with ideas of diversity in the definition of community. We need to accept that communities are active and developing within historical, political and material contexts; we need to understand that change is differentiated for different groupings by our systems and that communities are places of conflict and ambivalence which lack clarity. It is this call for the education system, and those within it to be proactive in understanding and including communities which comes through particularly loudly in Robin Richardson's chapter in Reader 1 (Chapter 24).

As Visser *et al.* state in their study of schools that are successfully coping with students with emotional and behavioural difficulties, 'schools need to be communities that are open, positive and diverse' (2002, p. 26). This openness stretches beyond the school walls, however, so that:

> Pupils were seen as part of a community which the school served ...
>
> [Staff] acknowledged that the solution to many emotional and behavioural difficulties lay outside of the school's ability to address fully.
>
> *(Visser* et al., *2002, p. 25)*

◯ Activity 14.6   Community values

· · · · · · · · · · · · · · · · · · · ·

Now read Chapter 24 in Reader 1. This is Robin Richardson's article, 'Unequivocal acceptance – lessons for education from the Stephen Lawrence Inquiry'. As you read this chapter think of examples of ways in which mainstream education's structures, practices and routines are racist. When you have done that, you may also wish to consider the ways in which they are sexist, homophobic, and disablist.

As you read the chapter by Robin Richardson you may have thought about the ways in which institutionalized racism may reflect an underlying racism in the wider community. This raises the question about whether reflecting the nature of the community is a suitable goal if that community is racist, sexist, homophobic, disablist, anti-inclusion and so on.

The education system can resist the values of the wider community, ignore their values, reflect their values or anticipate what their values could be. We would say that inclusion requires a respect for all aspects of the community, and this should therefore be demonstrated by the education system and those working within it; an equivalent respect should also be expected of anyone else who is involved with the system. If achieving this respect requires that we resist or ignore the values of others, then this can be considered to be part of the educative process, and therefore part of our open and active communication.

Shared values and language

Different underlying assumptions are bound to exist between groups and individuals and will come into conflict from time to time. Moderating that conflict will mean using a wide range of communication, administrative and interpersonal skills (Sproull, 1977), and this in turn calls for a common language and set of values so that people understand what is actually being dealt with and why. 'Talk is the resource that school personnel use to get others to act' (Gronn, 1983, p. 2).

A shared language is not just a means of overcoming conflict, of course. We use it to identify ourselves as parts of a culture (Zollers *et al.*, 1999), to develop shared meanings and to 'make sense' (Gronn, 1983). Zollers *et al.* found that within an inclusive setting people used language about support and being a resource for others. They used expressions of pride and ideas of unique school qualities, and talked about feeling safe and protected. Through talk the members of the school community were able to recognize that they shared their underlying assumptions and were part of the whole.

The importance of sharing language and values within the classroom is also clear. Without a common set of descriptive tools it is far harder for staff and students to work together or to discuss the processes in which and through which they are involved.

▷ Activity 14.7   Inclusive characteristics

Consider the ways in which the characteristics identified by Zollers *et al.* (leadership, a broad vision of school community, shared language and values) can be seen in the following quotation. This will be of use for your ECA where you are required to reflect on the viewpoint of someone you have interviewed:

> One head stated, 'We are a comprehensive school,' before stressing his duty to all children in his community, including those with learning and behavioural difficulties. In schools coping well with behavioural issues, statements such as this were an articulation of deeply held beliefs, and senior staff, imbued with inclusive values, possessed the skill and motivation to influence the attitudes and actions of their sometimes more-doubting colleagues.
>
> *(Cole, 2003, pp. 68–9)*

▷ We felt that the head teacher demonstrates a leadership committed to inclusion through publicly stating that he has this vision. His use of 'we' suggests a sense of being involved in a joint venture as a partner. The general commentary shows the importance of having shared values and beliefs and suggests that a senior management team can bring the rest of the staff to a position in which their values are changed. There is lacking – in this quote at least – a sense that leadership can be more broadly spread and come from the bottom up, and the notion that the community is not just about students.

5   How do we change the culture in practice?

Many inclusionists would advocate an immediate switch to an inclusive intake to schools. By this we mean that no school could refuse a pupil because of the way in which that pupil had been categorized. In this situation, most schools would have no choice but to change if they wished to offer improved, effective education. This understanding that a truly inclusive intake will drive change of systems and practices is one of the notions that underpins the Centre for Studies on Inclusive Education's *Inclusion Charter*. In their notes they point out that:

> In the Charter's vision of inclusion a restructured mainstream will change and adapt to accommodate diverse needs. A diverse mainstream would accept and cater for differences, not submerge, isolate or exclude them.

(CSIE, 2002)

As we have read in this and in previous units, however, there is considerable resistance to such a change from a variety of interested parties. Beyond this there is the additional resistance that greets any change, which is likely to be more intense as a result of top–down imposition. For this reason the CSIE talk about a gradual change within their charter. They see the need for allowing people and systems the time to change. In this section we will consider some of the methods that will encourage that change to take place and to do so effectively. We will consider the interplay between professional development, collaborative practice and the establishment of a learning community.

Professional development

One of the fundamental ways to change the system gradually is to develop appropriate teacher training and professional development. Andrew Kendrick (1995) evaluated the training of Scottish social workers and teachers. He suggests that negative stereotypes of each other's professions have been developed within initial training and that this level of mutual suspicion has been reinforced over the years because of lack of opportunities to find out about each other's work. Clearly, this will have a big impact, particularly since interpersonal relationships have been shown to be far more important to successful collaboration than formal processes (Jones, 2000).

At present, it is very unlikely that initial teacher training will be able to develop satisfactory understanding of the issues surrounding inclusive practice. It is a common complaint that inclusion and 'students with SEN' are paid scant attention (Lindsay and Dockrell, 2002). Christopher Robertson (1999) identifies constraints such as lack of time, option-based courses, poor linkage between schools and colleges and lack of practical advice. He highlights the requirements that teachers in initial training must demonstrate that they are familiar with the special educational needs (SEN) code of practice and must plan for and identify pupils with SEN, but other writers are very dismissive of these requirements. Margaret Reynolds, for example, says that 'they send powerful signals to beginning teachers that their professional life is grounded in the demonstration of explicit outcomes' (2001, p. 469). She calls for the TTA to 'include reference to the less tangible elements of performance' (p. 473) and directs them towards the characteristics identified by the Competences Working Group in Northern Ireland (DENI, 1993) which are 'caring for children, enthusiasm for teaching, commitment to reflective practice, commitment to equality of opportunity and recognition of the worth of the education of the whole child' (Reynolds, 2001, p. 471).

Despite the lack of impetus towards inclusion in the current training of teachers, it is possible that their subsequent continuing professional development (CPD) can improve things. CPD can help teachers to develop their reflection on their own practice, which can change their values and assumptions. The General Teaching Council in 2001 called for learning and development time for all teachers in their second and third years:

> The focus for these early years of professional development should be on engaging the individual teacher in reflection and action on pedagogy, the quality of learning, setting targets and high expectations, equal opportunities, planning, assessment and monitoring, curriculum and subject knowledge, and classroom management ... Team teaching, collaborative inquiry, observation and demonstration lessons would be among the means of encouraging this reflection and action.
>
> *(Berkeley, 2001, p. 509)*

Courses that encourage individuals to examine their attitudes and practices and which challenge their preconceptions and stereotypes can have a significant bearing on their culture and its inclusive practice. As Waterhouse (2002) demonstrates, teachers have a tendency to bracket individuals as 'insiders' or 'outsiders' and then to judge the propriety of their behaviour accordingly. Anything that reminds us of this process and that it can be controlled is likely to benefit the learning situation. Equality training is one technique for doing this. This can take a variety of forms, dealing with such issues as race, disability and sexual orientation.

As mentioned earlier, Parents for Inclusion feels strongly that the use of disability equality training has had a significant impact on the teachers they have worked with in Lambeth, and on the wider learning culture.

Professional development in later years is particularly likely to be valued if it is relevant to the teacher's context. Teachers are particularly enthusiastic about doing action research to seek better understanding of their practice, and about projects in which their voice is of significance. Dyson *et al.*, for example, noted that many teachers enjoyed training that was not about implementing a Government initiative: 'It's been wonderful to get involved in something which we haven't got to get involved in' (2002, p. 9). But they also noted that developments would have been unlikely in the schools involved in their research project if the LEA and their

University had not provided resources. This demonstrates the benefit of enhanced support and recognition for teacher research at a local and national level.

Collaboration across the boundaries

> The development of a collaborative ethos is a key feature. This entails collaboration within school, between staff and between staff and pupils, as well as with outside agencies.
>
> *(Visser et al., 2002, p. 26)*

Fundamental to the achievement of effective collaboration is the development of open communication within the immediate school community and beyond. This means, for example, that information about pupils' learning will be circulated (Florian and Rouse, 2001), staff will be receptive to management initiatives, and management will be supportive of ideas from teachers and other staff. Ted Cole (2003) refers to 'talking schools' where trust, respect, and common understanding lead to staff collaborating together.

We find calls for collaborative practice from many inclusionists and numerous examples of it in practice. Ainscow (1999) refers to collaborative enquiry and describes how he set up a research project in five schools using such an approach, which included staff, students, parents, LEA officers and governors. Peter Mittler (1999) highlights the need for teachers and other professionals to move beyond the child and to work in collaboration with the family. Jacquie Coulby and David Coulby (2001) describe the effective use of parents' groups to give them a voice within a primary school.

Ainscow and Howes (2001) argue for communities of practice, highlighting how LEAs can encourage 'networking at different levels within the service', noting in particular the success of links between head teachers. Brighouse and Woods (1999) see the importance of wider links in the successful development of practice in Birmingham. They highlight processes across a community which include professional development and management programmes, partnerships, consortia, databases of good practice, and sharing butterfly ideas (small changes that have disproportionate positive consequences). Within Scotland, the Network Development Groups (NDGs) have had a similar positive impact, as have the Local Education and Recreation Networks (LEARNs) that have been in place in Aberdeenshire.

This ability to call upon others is clearly of enormous value. Nind (2000), for example, describes how an individual operating as a 'critical friend' in a consultancy role can enable people 'to see their problem from a different perspective', contrasting their pragmatic need for a real and urgent solution with the critical friend's view of it as an intellectual challenge.

Efforts to maximize professional and parental involvement may be nullified if perspectives of children and young people are not included in the development of schools and other learning situations. For instance, counselling services may be very effective for some but to many refugee children they may seem entirely inappropriate (Rutter, 2001). Suzanne Mukherjee *et al.* (2000) give a typical example of a failure to communicate when they describe the teachers' perception of the school nurse as a 'useful source of emotional support' for students with a chronic health condition, even though:

> Young people themselves generally saw the school nurse as having a specific role to carry out health checks for all pupils, and not as someone to talk to about their particular health-related worries.
>
> *(Mukherjee et al., 2000, p. 66)*

Coulby and Coulby (2001) describe methods to encourage pupils' involvement in Batheaston Primary School; these methods include uses of a school council, an identified pupil with particular organizational responsibilities in the class each day, student awards for each other, pupil display areas and pupil self-assessment forms. They point out that such approaches are a consequence of walking 'the tightrope between the need for social control and conformity and the development of the full potential of each individual', but that such methods make it more likely that 'when we fall, it is in a particular direction' (p. 262).

All of the examples mentioned above are simple to establish and operate. They do not require huge amounts of money, nor do they require the development of a great many new skills. All they require is some organization and some time set aside within the working day. Staff will, of course, need to have the will to develop the few new skills and practices. As such, an open mind is useful, but if there are enough enthusiasts within the group then most closed minds will be encouraged to change.

Developing new ideas and ways of thinking

Successful change requires finding new ways of dealing with the old challenges as well as the new ones. Organizations that become more responsive and capable of adapting are sometimes called 'learning communities' or 'learning organizations'. In schools that are learning communities we would expect to find reviews as an active part of planning, and lessons being learned from different situations and applied elsewhere (Visser *et al.*, 2002). There would be a vision of actions, incidents and processes as being interconnected, a desire to come to terms with causes and consequences of situations, and an understanding that the context is an essential player in every event and decision.

The ability of a school community to be responsive is affected by its context. As Dyson *et al.* (2002) found in their study of eight schools developing inclusive practices, the attitude and commitment of the LEA were influential.

One of the advantages of the LEA focus is their understanding of the context of the school's operation. This notion of local context applies down to the level of the individual classroom. Dyson *et al.* (2002) highlight the importance of allowing teachers to exercise judgement to use the current system to better meet pupil 'need'. They recommend allowing schools to create 'spaces' for change in order to maximize pupil participation and learning, They also point out that teachers still have 'a reserve of commitment to a particular kind of professionalism that in recent years has been somewhat undervalued and which could provide, if nurtured, a stimulus to the development of practice in schools' (p. 10).

There is a clear-cut benefit that comes from teachers and other staff taking time for reflection and enquiry, to explore their own practice and the practice of those with whom they work (Ainscow, 1999; Brighouse and Woods, 1999; Hopkins, 2001) and in being supported in their questioning by others with experience in reflective practice. Within this process there is room for traditional research models, and for use of methods such as action research, in which teachers use reflection and innovation systematically and strategically to develop their understanding and practice. It can involve widespread and systematic collection and use of data, with strategies for review and interpretation, but it also calls for more immediate analysis, a reflexivity in the moment, when the teacher considers what is happening and the role of themselves and others within that moment.

Encouraging reflection is also at the core of a number of models of interaction that will be of use in the inclusive classroom, such as 'intensive interaction' (Nind and Hewitt, 1988), 'connective pedagogy' (Corbett and Norwich, 1999, cited in Corbett, 2001), and 'innovative thinking' (Hart, 1996) (these were explored in Unit 13). These reflective and reflexive approaches are taken up by other writers in suggesting ways to open up our thinking about learning. Mike Blamires (1999), for example, sees innovative thinking as essential to allowing learning situations to provide multiple opportunities for alternative presentations of content, of self-expression and for engagement and motivation.

Ainscow (1998) particularly wants to encourage reflection within educational settings, stating that from his own experience teachers' development is more effective when based on consideration of their own practice than when they apply others' research. It is also an approach which ties in with the ideas of professional development and collaboration raised above. It is not a difficult step, for example, for schools and LEAs to make research part of job descriptions or essential components of professional development plans, or to encourage applications for funding.

◯ Activity 14.8   Change in an LEA

Now find the interview with Helen Jenner on Video Band A. Helen Jenner works for Tower Hamlets Local Education Authority. As you view this interview, consider her comments about the approach of the LEA and individuals within the borough in relation to change. Think about some of the processes she describes the LEA undergoing in its attempts to achieve a change in borough's culture.

Becoming learning communities

The notion of the learning organization and learning community was popularized by Peter Senge (1990 and 2000), who outlined five components of such groups. Fundamental to this is attempting a shift of mind from viewing parts to viewing wholes, seeing people as active participants rather than as merely reactive.

- Personal mastery – developing and deepening a personal vision, seeking objectivity and a belief in the ability to make a difference.
- Mental models – understanding the way you and others in the group think and reason, your assumptions and generalizations.
- Building shared vision – aligning aims and ambitions around a common identity and understanding.
- Team learning – working with others in the group to move beyond your own ways of seeing, suspending assumptions and thinking together.
- Systems thinking – recognizing your own work as part of the system's larger whole and how each aspect affects what goes on elsewhere.

Senge acknowledges the need for there to be enough people who share the mental models and for people who can clearly demonstrate the models. These can act as a catalyst for others' change as well as their own.

We hope you will recognize that Senge's model has much in common with the descriptions in this course of schools that are genuinely striving for inclusion. In Unit 9 we described our vision as the creation of a community of learners who are independent, active, participatory and equal. We said that to create such communities we will have to challenge existing structures and hierarchies to become open, participatory and flexible, and to believe in and make a commitment to respecting the differences of others . As Brighouse and Woods (1999) note, in their experience pupils and staff in successful schools treat each other with equal respect; staff are positive about each other's achievements, resist public criticism of each other and take the same approach to pupil behaviour. Visser *et al.* (2002) note that in schools that are successful in dealing with pupils with BESD, 'Staff ... modelled ways of coping with the strains and stresses of school life' (p. 25). As we mentioned above, such schools have a collaborative approach, involving as many people as possible, and are willing to examine practice:

> As well as being 'talking' schools, they are 'learning' schools using the 'do-review-learn-apply' planning and practice cycle in most aspects of school life (Dennison and Kirk 1990) including behaviour management. Practitioners were engaged in an on-going re-evaluation of their work through formal development days, training and advice from LEA support services or through staff working groups. Lessons learnt led to adjusted practice ...
>
> *(Cole, 2003, p. 69)*

Making sure that a school is a learning community may take the sort of shift in culture that we are saying is often needed to generate inclusive practice. It will require people to collaborate, to reflect and to change accordingly. By introducing the concept we do not bring ourselves any closer to achieving that cultural shift. However, there is a tool which can help people describe change: systems thinking. This is a language used to think and talk about complex issues. It encourages people to consider the degree to which they are part of the whole and how they can take their involvement further. If we use the model, we must ask questions of ourselves and consider our position within the whole and in relation to the whole.

There are other models which can help us to consider the degree to which we are involved and responsive. The *Index for Inclusion* (Booth and Ainscow, 2002) includes over 140 questions to indicate whether a school is moving towards an inclusive culture and inclusive values. Dyson *et al.* (2002) talk about their use of success criteria and success indicators to help identify when positive change has occurred. They used the following questions to guide their investigation:

- What are the barriers to participation and learning experienced by students?

- What practices can help to overcome these barriers?

- To what extent do such practices facilitate improved learning outcomes?

- How can such practices be encouraged and sustained within LEAs and schools?

Ainscow (1999) talks about establishing the following four principles to guide a process of enquiry:

- Is it of direct help to people in the schools visited?
- Does it inform the development of policy elsewhere?
- Does it demonstrate rigour such that the findings would be worthy of wider attention?
- Does it inform the thinking of the team members?

If a school draws upon such questions as these, using them to help generate personal mastery and mental models and build a shared vision, it is more likely to achieve a collaborative, learning approach that will build an inclusive school where the whole is greater than its individual parts, but in which none of those individuals are forgotten. Through this process there can be a movement towards change that comes from everyone within the school community, because the effort has been directed towards including them all:

> But the top driving it won't get anything done. I guarantee you, if teachers aren't on board, forget it. Just as much so, in the school, you've got to get parents on board, at least enough of them, and enough of the teachers. And ultimately, I think the most important leadership often will come from kids. It's not top down in the traditional sense; it says that all the critical roles of a system have important leadership responsibilities, including the kids.
>
> *(Peter Senge, quoted in Newcomb, 2003)*

◯ Activity 14.9   Cycles and stages

Consider Figure 14.3, a model of the learning cycle. Consider the way in which you approach complex problems. Do you consciously or subconsciously go through these stages? Do you feel that all situations require a structured analysis such as this? Do you approach problems in an intuitive way? Are there ways in which such a cycle can be of use retrospectively? Should there be a difference between an organizational response and an individual response? Discuss these questions with a friend or colleague. Search out the values and the contradictions that exist in using a model to achieve inclusive practice.

Implement improvements
Make new predictions
More complex tasks
Re-use and transfer information
Employ new ideas
Use learning to improve work

Active, independent and collaborative work
Experiment with ideas
Gather information
Facilitate basic tasks
Explore and predict
Trial and error

Make judgements
Reach conclusions
Formulate answers
Absorb information
Develop new ideas
Extract and internalize meaning from work

Reflect upon and discuss practical work
Share and compare ideas
Check, select and reject information
Frame questions
Analyse and interpret results
Identify improvements

Figure 14.3   Stages in a learning cycle (adapted by Taylor, 2000).

6 Conclusion

As Clark *et al.* (1999) point out, we have to struggle to create inclusive education. We have to deal with widespread resistance, conflicting policy initiatives, continuing segregation in special schools, and a limited understanding of inclusive technology, methods and principles. The fundamental change requires a change in the cultures of our learning environments. The practical methods that can achieve this shift in culture are available to us, however, and importantly they are flexible so as to be appropriate for the context of the school which is applying them. Through a combination of legislative pressure, professional development, equality training, and support for research we can encourage reflection and the understanding of learning contexts. By supporting the autonomy of individuals, while establishing broad communities of learning in schools and between schools, we can call upon the breadth of experience, skills and facilities of all those within the learning situation and across education authorities to develop new practices and understandings. By embracing new school policies, setting targets in context and establishing principles we can encourage all of us to talk to each other, to learn and to apply that learning.

References

Ainscow, M. (1995) 'Special needs through school improvement; school improvement through special needs' in Clarke, C., Dyson, A., and Millward, A. (eds) *Towards Inclusive Schools*, London, David Fulton, pp. 63–77.

Ainscow, M. (1998) 'Would it work in theory? Arguments for practitioner research and theorising in the special needs field' in Clarke, C., Dyson, A., and Millward, A. (eds) *Theorising Special Education*, London, Routledge, pp. 7–20.

Ainscow, M. (1999) *Understanding the Development of Inclusive Schools*, London, Falmer Press.

Ainscow, M. and Howes, A. (2001) 'LEAs and school improvement: what is it that makes the difference?' Paper presented at the British Education Research Association annual conference, University of Leeds, 13–15 September, 2001.

Ainscow, M., Farrell, P., Tweddle, D., and Malki, G. (1999) 'The role of LEAs in developing inclusive policies and practices', *British Journal of Special Education*, **26**(3), pp. 136–40.

Barbara Priestman School (2003) 'Our school'. Available from http://www.barbara-priestman.org.uk/home.htm [accessed March 2004].

Berkeley, R. (2001) 'Empowerment and professionalism: the General Teaching Council for England – developing policy to support social inclusion', *Journal of In-service Education*, **27**(3), pp. 501–14.

Bishop, A. and Jones, P. (2002) 'Promoting inclusive practice in primary initial teacher training: influencing hearts as well as minds', *Support for Learning*, **17**(2), pp. 58–63.

Blamires, M. (1999) 'Universal design for learning: re-establishing differentiation as part of the inclusion agenda?', *Support for Learning*, **14**(4), pp. 158–63.

Booth, A. and Ainscow, M. (2002) *Index for Inclusion: developing learning and participation in schools*, Bristol, CSIE.

Brighouse, T. and Woods, D. (1999) *How to Improve your School*, London, RoutledgeFalmer.

Centre for Studies on Inclusive Education (CSIE) (2002) *The Inclusion Charter*, Bristol, CSIE. Available from http://inclusion.uwe.ac.uk/csie/charter.htm [accessed April 2003].

Clarke, C., Dyson, A., Millward, A., and Robson, S. (1999) 'Theories of inclusion, theories of schools: deconstructing and reconstructing the "inclusive school"', *British Educational Research Journal*, **25**(2), pp. 157–77.

Cole, T. (2003) 'Policies for positive behaviour management' in Tilstone, C. and Rose, R. (eds) *Strategies to Promote Inclusive Practice*, London, RoutledgeFalmer, pp. 67–83.

Corbett, J. (2001) *Supporting Inclusive Education: a connective pedagogy*, London, RoutledgeFalmer.

Coulby, J. and Coulby, D. (2001) 'Pupil participation in the social and education processes of a primary school' in Wearmouth, J. (ed.) *Special Educational Provision in the Context of Inclusion – policy and practice in schools*, London, David Fulton in association with The Open University, pp. 245–63.

Croll, P. and Moses, D. (2000) 'Ideologies and utopias: education professionals' views of inclusion', *European Journal of Special Educational Needs*, **15**(1), pp. 1–12.

Crow, G. and Allan, G. (1994) *Community Life*, London, Harvester Wheatsheaf.

Deal, T. (1985) 'Cultural change: opportunity, silent killer, or metamorphosis?' in Kilmann, R., Saxton, M., and Serpa, R. (eds) *Gaining Control of the Corporate Culture*, San Francisco, Jossey-Bass.

Dennison, B. and Kirk, R. (1990) *Do, Review, Learn, Apply: a simple guide to experiential learning*, Oxford, Blackwell.

Department for Education and Employment (DfEE)(2000) *The Role of the Local Education Authority in School Education*, London, DfEE.

Department for Education and Skills (DfES) (2002) *The Distribution of Resources to Support Inclusion*, London, DfES.

Department of Education for Northern Ireland (DENI) (1993) *Competences: Report of Working Group 1, Review of Initial Teacher Training in Northern Ireland, Consultation Paper*, Bangor (NI), DENI.

Dyson, A., Gallannaugh, F., and Millward, A. (2002) 'Making space in the standards agenda: developing inclusive practices in schools', paper presented at the European Conference on Educational Research, University of Lisbon, 11–14 September 2002.

Elmore, R. (1995) 'Teaching, learning, and school organization: principles of practice and the regularities of schooling', *Educational Administration Quarterly*, **31**(3), pp. 355–74.

Florian, L. and Rouse, M. (2001) 'Inclusive practice in English secondary schools: lessons learned', *Cambridge Journal of Education*, **31**(3), pp. 399–412.

Forlin, C., Douglas, G. and Hattie, J. (1996) 'Inclusive practices: how accepting are our teachers?', *International Journal of Disability, Development and Education*, **43**, pp. 119–33.

Fullan, M. (1991) *The New Meaning of Educational Change*, London, Cassell.

Gronn, P. (1983) 'Talk as the work: the accomplishment of school administration', *Administrative Science Quarterly*, **28**, pp. 1–21.

Hart, S. (1996) *Beyond Special Needs: enhancing children's learning through innovative thinking*, London, Paul Chapman Publishing.

Hopkins, D. (2001) *School Improvement for Real*, London, RoutledgeFalmer.

Johnson, G. (1992) 'Managing strategic change – strategy, culture and action', *Long Range Planning*, **25**(1), pp. 28–36.

Jones, H. (2000) 'Partnerships: a common sense approach to inclusion?', paper presented at the Standing Conference on University Teaching and Research (SCUTREA), 30th Annual Conference, 3–5 July 2000, University of Nottingham.

Kendrick, A. (1995) 'Supporting families through inter-agency work: youth strategies in Scotland' in Hill, M., Kirk, R., and Part, D. (eds) *Supporting Families*, Edinburgh, HMSO.

Kilmann, R., Saxton, M., and Serpa, R. (1985) 'Introduction: five key issues in understanding and changing culture' in Kilmann, R., Saxton, M., and Serpa, R. (eds) *Gaining Control of the Corporate Culture*, San Francisco, Jossey-Bass.

Lindsay, G. and Dockrell, J. (2002) 'Meeting the needs of children with special language and communication needs: a critical perspective on inclusion and collaboration', *Child Language Teaching and Therapy*, **18**(2), pp. 91–101.

Martin, I. (2000) 'Re-theorizing "community": towards a dialectical understanding of inclusion', paper presented at the Standing Conference on University Teaching and Research (SCUTREA), 30th Annual Conference, 3–5 July 2000, University of Nottingham.

Mittler, P. (1999) *Working towards Inclusive Education – social contexts*, London, David Fulton.

Mukherjee, S., Lightfoot, J., and Sloper, P. (2000) 'The inclusion of pupils with a chronic health condition in mainstream school: what does it mean for teachers?' *Educational Research*, **42**(1), pp. 59–72.

Newcomb, A. (2003) 'Peter Senge on organizational learning', *The School Administrator Web Edition*. Available at: http://www.aasa.org/publications/sa/2003_05/SengeQ&A.htm [accessed 25 April 2003].

Nind, M. (2000) 'What about child development and developmental approaches?', Cardiff, BERA Conference.

Nind, M. and Hewitt, D.(1988) 'Interaction as curriculum: a process method in a school for pupils with severe learning difficulties', *British Journal of Special Education*, **15**, pp. 53–7.

Reynolds, M. (2001) 'Education for inclusion, teacher education and the Teacher Training Agency standards', *Journal of In-Service Education*, **27**(3), pp. 465–76.

Robertson, C. (2002) 'Initial teacher education and inclusive schooling', *Support for Learning*, **14**(4), pp. 169–73.

Rutter, J. (2001) 'Supporting refugee children in 21st century Britain: a compendium of essential information', Stoke-on-Trent, Trentham Books.

Schein, E. H. (1984) 'Coming to a new awareness of organizational culture', *Sloan Management Review*, **25**(2), pp. 3–17.

Scruggs, T. and Mastropieri, M. (1996) 'Teacher perceptions of mainstreaming/inclusion, 1958–1995: a research synthesis', *Exceptional Children*, **63**(1), pp. 59–74.

Senge, P. (1990) *The Fifth Discipline: the art and practice of the learning organization*, New York, Doubleday Books.

Senge, P. (2000) *Schools That Learn: a fifth discipline fieldbook for educators, parents, and everyone who cares about education*, New York, Doubleday Books.

Skrtic, T. and Sailor, W. (1996) 'School linked services integration: crisis and opportunity in the transition to post-modern society', *Remedial and Special Education*, 17(5), pp. 271–84.

Slee, R. and Weiner, G. (2001) 'Education reform and reconstructions as a challenge to research genres: reconsidering school effectiveness research and inclusive schooling', *School Effectiveness and School Improvement*, 12(1), pp. 83–98.

Sproull, L. (1977) 'Building an ethical school: a theory for practice', *Educational Administration Quarterly*, 27, pp. 185–202.

Squires, D. A. and Kranyik, R. D. (1996) 'The Comer Program: changing school culture', *Educational Leadership*, January, pp. 29–32.

Taylor, P. (2000) 'Tools for learning', *Literacy Today*, 25. Available from: http://www.literacytrust.org.uk/Pubs/philtaylor.html [accessed 25 April 2003].

Visser, J., Cole, T., and Daniels, H. (2002) 'Inclusion for the difficult to include', *Support for Learning*, 17(1), pp. 23–6.

Vlachou, A. (1997) *Struggles for Inclusive Education*, Buckingham, Open University Press.

Wallace, M. and Pocklington, K. (2002) *Managing Complex Educational Change – a large scale reorganization of schools*, London, Routledge-Falmer.

Waterhouse, S. (2002) 'Deviant and non-deviant identities in the classroom: patrolling the boundaries of the normal social world', paper presented at the European Conference on Education Research, University of Lisbon, 11–14 September 2002.

Zollers, N. J., Ramanathan, A. K., and Yu, M. (1999) 'The relationship between school culture and inclusion: how an inclusive culture supports inclusive education', *Qualitative Studies in Education*, 12(2), pp. 157–74.

UNIT 15   Agenda for change

Prepared for the course team by Katy Simmons and Melanie Nind

Contents

1 Introduction

Whatever you do may seem insignificant, but it is most important that you do it.

(*Mahatma Ghandi*)

In this unit we look at the part played by individual activists, families and groups in 'making inclusion happen' both at national and at local level. For some, the commitment to inclusion has been a long-term campaign, based on their own early experiences in segregated settings. Jane Campbell, for example, wrote:

> I am a whole hearted supporter and campaigner for the total integration of disabled children into mainstream schools and have been since the grand age of seven.
>
> You may think that seven is a very early age to be aware of one's educational and social deprivation, but you have to believe me when I say that by that small age I was displaying the usual symptoms of someone who is ashamed or frustrated with their situation regarding school. I hated the school bus because it took me away from my local friends, who were beginning to wonder why I didn't go to school with them. It also highlighted my differences at a time that I desperately wanted to do/be the same ...
>
> I am grown up now (so they keep telling me), but I still feel anger about those days, and *I am not alone*.
>
> (*Campbell quoted in Rieser and Mason, 1992, p. 168*)

Human rights principles, often developed as a result of childhood experiences, underpin the efforts of many campaigners to break down barriers in education. As a young child, Mark Vaughan, co-director of the Centre for Studies on Inclusive Education (CSIE), attended Summerhill School, the progressive residential school founded by A. S. Neill in 1921, where pupils' freedom to participate was central to the work of the school. Later on he experienced 'segregated' education as an 11+ 'failure'. Both experiences fuelled his commitment to inclusion:

> [I]n 1982 when I first established CSIE, I estimate there were about ten of us in the UK who were willing to promote the basic human rights principles and philosophy underpinning integration.
>
> (*Vaughan, 2002, p. 44*)

Others have turned into 'activists for inclusion' as a result of their experiences as parents. Wendy Crane's experience was sudden and brutal, when her son Niki was refused a mainstream secondary school place:

> Yes, it's all very strange ... You spend all this time working with the teachers to prepare your son for the big school, the school all his friends are going to and then at the last minute the rug is pulled, in our case right from under us. I mean why allow a child to go to a mainstream school if afterwards he's going to be carted off to somewhere special?

(Crane quoted in Brandon, 1997, p. 15)

In this unit we look at the different kinds of activism that have helped to put inclusion on the national agenda and at some of the groups and individuals who have contributed – and continue to contribute – to bringing about change. Some activists have challenged existing systems through the law, some through direct action. Some have set up alternative structures to include potentially marginalized young people. Some have worked for change from within structures, such as national charities. Some of the changes they have brought about have been reflected in legislation and have therefore had a broad impact: others have been local *causes célèbres*, not always with successful outcomes, that have nevertheless contributed to a climate where change has been possible.

Many changes in the law have focused on young people legally defined as 'having special educational needs' or as being 'disabled', and much of this unit will focus on them. Nonetheless, we maintain our broader view of inclusion as a wider social process that challenges marginalization and aims to increase the participation and power of all marginalized groups. Some legal changes, in particular in the area of school exclusion, have made marginalization more likely for some pupils. This process is likely to continue: head teachers in Scotland, for example, have pressed for increased exclusion rights for schools, with the 'needs of the majority' to take precedence over the 'rights of the few' (Munro, 2003).

We look at the way that disability activists have defined much of the agenda for change and at how that has affected others who are also 'on the margins'. We conclude that there is still a long way to go before full participation is achieved, but that activists of all kinds continue to struggle against compromise and against competing agendas to make inclusion happen.

The unit aims to:

- examine the different forms that activism takes;
- consider the local and national impact that different forms of activism have had;
- look at where change may come from in the future.

Learning outcomes

By the end of this unit you will have:

- developed an understanding of the part played by individuals and groups in bringing about changes in national and local practice;
- reflected on some of the barriers that individuals and groups have had to overcome in order to bring about change;
- considered where changes need to come in the future.

Resources for this unit

For Activity 15.5 you will need to read:

- Chapter 7, 'Inclusion – looking forward' by Carol Boys, in Reader 1.

You will need to have access to Unit 4. Internet access would also be helpful.

2 Struggling with the law: challenges to Section 316

A focus for change

In this section we see how one part of the law, Section 316 of the 1996 Education Act, became a focus for lobbying and how it was subsequently amended. This gave children a better chance of an inclusive education, but conceded to campaigners only a part of what they had demanded. The story of Section 316 is an example of how individual experiences contribute to the developing impetus for change, change that is often incremental rather than conclusive.

The 1981 Education Act, which became law in 1983, placed on LEAs in England a 'qualified' legal duty to offer places in mainstream schools to children defined in law as having 'special educational needs'. The legal duty was, however, dependent on a number of conditions, all of which were set out in what eventually became Section 316 of the 1996 Education Act. Section 316 was a source of great difficulty for many families and the focus of challenge from many campaigners.

Section 316 reads as follows:

(1)   Any person exercising any functions under this Part in respect of a child with special educational needs who should be educated in a school shall secure that, if the conditions mentioned in sub-section (2) are satisfied, the child is educated in a school which is not a special school unless that is incompatible with the wishes of his parent.

(2)   The conditions are that educating the child in a school which is not a special school is compatible with:

(a)   his receiving the special educational provision which his learning difficulty calls for,

(b)   the provision of efficient education for the children with whom he will be educated, and

(c)   the efficient use of resources.

Section 316 allowed those empowered to make decisions about mainstream placements, whether they were LEA officers, Special Educational Needs (SEN) Tribunal panels or High Court judges, to block such placements by invoking one of more of these conditions (generally referred to as 'the caveats'). Furthermore, the 'mainstream/special' decision was the only decision in the area of special education where relative costs could be invoked as part of the decision-making process. Many parents, having established that the mainstream school they preferred could meet their child's needs, found themselves unable to counter the argument that it would cost more to send their child there.

Families in dispute

Many families found that their challenge to Section 316 took them into long-term disputes with their LEAs. One such family, the Gibbs family from Suffolk, faced a court appearance as a result of their commitment to the inclusion of their daughter Emma. Emma Gibbs, one of seven children with Down syndrome adopted or fostered by Madge and Bob Gibbs, had attended her local primary school. When it came to secondary transfer, the Gibbs expected that she would move, along with the other children from her village, to neighbouring Stradbroke High School. However, the LEA, as it was entitled to do under Section 316, decided that Emma should attend a special school 30 miles away from her home. The Gibbses refused to send her there and Emma was out of school for three years. Eventually, shortly before Emma reached statutory school-leaving age, the Gibbses were prosecuted for Emma's non-attendance at school. In the newsletter of the Independent Panel for Special Education Advice (IPSEA), the Gibbses explained their position as follows:

> It is crucially important for young people with Down's Syndrome to have appropriate models of peer group behaviour and these are not provided, in general, by children in special schools.

> We do not believe that a young person should have to travel some 60 miles a day, every day of their school life, to go to school. There is no way that Emma would have stood up to this stress ... We have had first hand

experience of the effects of such protracted travelling on a young person ... in the case of our son.

(IPSEA, 1994, p. 2)

The Gibbses' story received national attention: *The Observer*, for example, reported on the 'thousands of pounds of tax payers' money' being spent on the prosecution of the Gibbses by Suffolk LEA, pointing out that Madge and Bob Gibbs could face a prison sentence if convicted (Hugill, 1993, p. 3).

Eventually, their case was adjourned: Emma never returned to school but went to a local college. The Gibbses' struggles continued with their younger children. They later reported that their son Paul, after a year out of school and after being featured in a TV programme highlighting his case, had been admitted to Stradbroke High School. They wrote:

> As parents who have been fighting for inclusive education for our children for some ten years, we are very pleased with this outcome and sincerely hope that the actions we have taken over the years may change attitudes and encourage others who feel as we do.

(IPSEA, 1997a, p. 11)

But their struggle was being repeated in other parts of the country. Joanne Spendiff, from Wallsend, for example, had attended a local primary school. Like Emma Gibbs, Joanne faced barriers to her transfer to secondary school. Her parents expressed a preference for their local Catholic high school, but their LEA named a special school and invoked all three of the caveats from Section 316 to justify their decision. The LEA said that the preferred school could not meet Joanne's needs, her placement at the school would be detrimental to the education of other children and that it would be an inefficient use of the council's resources.

At the tribunal which followed, the LEA's evidence was limited: it emerged that it had not even consulted the family's preferred school, making its assertion that the school could not meet Joanne's needs, seem, in the family's view, flawed. But although the Spendiffs presented evidence in all three areas covered by the caveats, their appeal to the Tribunal was unsuccessful, as was their subsequent appeal to the High Court (Simmons, 2000).

Direct action

At the same time that the Spendiffs were mounting their legal challenge to Section 316, the Crane family in Preston were also in dispute with their LEA. Niki Crane's struggle to be included at his local secondary school involved not only the law but also direct action by activists supporting the family. In *The Invisible Wall: Niki's fight to be included*, Stewart Brandon details both aspects of the struggle. The story is a dramatic one, during which 'education professionals' John Kenworthy and Joe Whittaker from the Bolton Institute made the decision to '"stop hiding behind our salaries" to actually put ourselves on the line for the people we were trying to help' (Brandon, 1997, p. 43). 'Putting themselves on the line' led to an occupation of County Hall in Preston and forcible eviction from the boardroom by security guards. Joe Whittaker tells the story:

> It was real 'keystone cops' stuff, them running round and round the table, me and John dodging their tackles till finally this big oaf got hold of me real tight. I couldn't shake him off so I clung on to a table leg and held on for dear life ... I lost my grip and they dragged me off. They had got John, he was being marched down stairs ... Before I knew what was happening, John had broken free again and was racing back up the stairs ... We got back into the boardroom and resumed the chase ... that's when I think it happened. I felt so light headed, dizzy and strange and then I was falling, falling for ever down into God knows where. That's the last thing I remember, till I came round in the ambulance and heard the awful sound of the sirens.
>
> *(Whittaker quoted in Brandon, 1997, pp. 47–8)*

Joe Whittaker's collapse proved to be diabetes-related, and he was soon encamped again with John Kenworthy, this time outside County Hall. The conflict continued, with arrest for breach of the peace, followed by fines and subsequent court appearances when the fines were not paid.

> The magistrate reprimanded both men and reminded them that they would go to prison if they didn't pay. Joe and John explained that they would not pay in protest over 'segregation in Lancashire's education system'.
>
> *(Brandon, 1997, p. 60)*

Following tumultuous scenes, during which Joe Whittaker called out 'Why weren't the education department on trial today?', 'What had happened to the rights of ordinary people, in a system like this?', 'Why couldn't kids go to school?' (Brandon, 1997, p. 63), he was sentenced to seven days' imprisonment for contempt of court.

Later, the Cranes used their appeal rights at the SEN Tribunal to challenge Lancashire's decision. Not only that appeal, but also the family's subsequent appeal to the High Court, was unsuccessful.

For the Gibbses, the Spendiffs and the Cranes, challenge to their LEAs took a very long time. All the families were supported by voluntary organizations, with legal teams acting on a voluntary basis and, in the case of the Spendiffs and Cranes, by the Barrow Cadbury Trust, a charitable trust with an interest in social issues and in the development of the law. However, campaigners were beginning to accept that progress via the existing law was unlikely. Writing about the Cranes' case, John Wright from the voluntary organization IPSEA commented: 'it is difficult to avoid the conclusion that the law on inclusion does not work' (IPSEA, 1997b, p. 13).

Activity 15.1   Personal challenges

Talk to a colleague or another course member about what you would have found the most difficult part of what the Gibbses, the Spendiffs and the Cranes did. Do you think, in the same circumstances, you would have done what they did? What impact do you think such a struggle might have had on you personally?

All the families were involved in protracted disputes, during which their children were out of school. The families had to organize home education for extended periods and, in the case of the Gibbses, had to face legal action against them by their LEA. Both families were featured in the local and national press. The Cranes watched their supporters become involved in violent scenes and eventually in dramatic court appearances. The legal processes themselves were complex and required professional and potentially expensive legal advice. The Spendiffs and Cranes were only able to continue their challenge because of solicitors and barristers working *pro bono* (for free), in the interests of justice.

The practical difficulties of challenging decisions were considerable – it was not easy, for example, to get details of relative costs or details of what schools might provide.

Even after considerable, lengthy struggle, there was no guarantee of success. Emma Gibbs never experienced secondary school; Joanne Spendiff was offered a mainstream school place, but in a neighbouring LEA. Niki Crane never went to Tarleton High School.

You might also have thought about who were the winners and who were the losers in these stories. Maybe you decided that the long-term benefits outweighed the stresses and difficulties. Certainly these cases raised the profile of the issues and in a long-term sense improved the opportunities of children coming after them. You will have formed your own view on whether, for you, these gains made the struggle worthwhile.

The amendment of Section 316

High-profile cases such as those we have described served to underline the unsatisfactory nature of Section 316. Consequently, when new legislation was proposed to amend the existing legal framework of special education law, Section 316 became a focus for lobbying by the voluntary sector.

In its response to government consultation, IPSEA commented that the third caveat (efficient use of resources) was, in their experience, the one most commonly cited by LEAs, who then used cost issues to deny inclusion. However, in IPSEA's view, the best way forward would be to scrap all the caveats:

> IPSEA has argued for some time now for all caveats to be removed and for children with special educational needs to have their education provided for, including their special educational needs, in mainstream schools where this is the parent's wish ... IPSEA does not advocate the use by schools of their temporary and permanent exclusion powers in relation to children with special educational needs ... but this particular argument does require us to remind the Government that these powers are in place, and are extensively used by schools when believed to be necessary. Removing all three caveats, therefore, would not pose a threat to other pupils' welfare or education which schools would be unable to deal with.
>
> *(IPSEA, 2003)*

This position was shared by the Special Educational Consortium, an umbrella body representing large numbers of disability, parent and children's organizations. Since schools already had the means to deal with children who were disruptive, campaigners argued that they did not need the erection of additional barriers to mainstream placements.

When Baroness Blackstone introduced the Special Educational Needs and Disability Bill into the House of Lords in December 2000, she spoke about how the Government saw inclusion:

> The Government's commitment to inclusion has been strong and constant. We are committed to ensuring that children with special educational needs are included wherever possible. The potential social, moral and educational benefits are significant ... Our approach is pragmatic and practical, recognising ... that there is a continuing and vital role for special schools ...
>
> [I]nclusion does not mean that every child should be placed in a mainstream school irrespective of their needs and circumstances. There will be cases, particularly where there is severe challenging behaviour, where a

mainstream place is not appropriate. But that will be a small minority of pupils. We believe that many more pupils could and should benefit from a mainstream place where this is what their parents want. But we also believe that pupils should be protected from those whose inclusion would adversely affect either their learning or their safety.

(Hansard, 2000, column 635)

The Government, clearly, was not persuaded that all the caveats should go and proposed amended legislation that would remove all the caveats except the one referring to the 'provision of efficient education for the children with whom he will be educated' (1996 Education Act, Section 316, 2(b)).

As Brian Lamb, chair of the Special Education Consortium, pointed out, they had become 'nervous about the reaction of the teacher unions' to the removal of all the caveats (Lamb, 2001).

In the Special Educational Needs and Disability Act 2001, the amended Section 316 said that a child with a statement:

> must be educated in a mainstream school unless that is incompatible with:
>
> (a)   the wishes of his parents, or
> (b)   the provision of efficient education for other children.

During the parliamentary debate on this issue, there were many objections to this amendment. In the Lords, Lord Rix commented that:

> Interpretation of 'efficient education' is notoriously subjective and as a consequence this still leaves open the potential for discrimination.

(Hansard, 2000, column 651)

Lord Ashley, another long-term campaigner, commented that:

> Exemption has been abused in the past and there is no doubt that it will be abused again in the future, to the detriment of the child.

(Hansard, 2000, column 656)

But, in the end, a compromise was accepted and the 'efficient education' caveat stayed. Brian Lamb commented:

> The SEN lobby remains deeply suspicious that the efficient education of other children will be used by less committed or cash-strapped authorities to divert children from mainstream provision.

(Lamb, 2001)

Activity 15.2   Question time

Look again at Baroness Blackstone's speech that introduced the Special Needs and Disability Bill into the House of Lords (at the beginning of this sub-section). Imagine you are interviewing Baroness Blackstone after she made this speech. Draft four questions that you would like to ask her. This activity will help you with the examinable component of this course.

The questions you ask will, of course, depend on your own developing perspectives on inclusion. You might want to explore Baroness Blackstone's own conceptualization of inclusion, as reflected in the language she uses. Or you might want to seek practical illustrations of some of the points she makes. Our questions included the following:

- What do you mean by 'wherever possible'?
- Who decides when inclusion is 'possible'?
- Do you think all children should have a legal right to be included?
- What is the difference between 'what parents want' and the rights of the child?
- Does your use of the word 'protected' suggest that we need to be afraid of children who might be 'different'?
- What do you mean by 'pragmatic and practical'?
- How do we define 'severe challenging behaviour'?

The story of the amendment of Section 316 shows how campaigning for change can take many different forms. Eventually, with Section 316, inclusion activists of all kinds reached the same conclusion – that existing legislation did not work and that amendment was necessary. The process of amendment required lobbying and briefing of members of both Houses of Parliament, but the final amendment remained a compromise, since other powerful 'stakeholders', in particular teachers' unions, were also lobbying with different agendas.

You may recall that Richard Rieser, whose Chapter 16 in Reader 1 you read as part of Unit 4, wrote with some satisfaction of the impact of the Alliance for Inclusive Education on the amended legislation. But Brian Lamb (2001) described the acceptance of the remaining caveat as 'an accommodation between the lobby and the Government'. For some members of the lobby, including the Alliance, that 'accommodation' was brief. Just over a year after the amendment to Section 316 came into force, the Government launched a consultation on the future role of special schools, based on a report by the Special

Schools Working Group. In a preface to the Report, the government minister who had commissioned it wrote:

> Special schools ... form a key and important part of the overall provision available for children with special educational needs ... The Government is strongly committed to the sector and wants to work in partnership with them to ensure they have a secure long-term future [...]
>
> The special schools sector enjoys the Government's full support.
>
> *(DFES, 2003)*

In a press release headed 'Government breaks promises on inclusion for disabled children', the Alliance for Inclusive Education, along with CSIE and other campaigning inclusion groups, registered a strong protest against the Report.

> A new DfES report completely undermines the Government's long-standing promise of greater equality for disabled children. The report misrepresents what inclusion is, and how to achieve it, by recommending a permanent role to segregated schooling.
>
> *(Parents for Inclusion, 2003)*

The debate – if it had ever ended – had started again.

Activity 15.3   Power and influence

A number of different groups of people, with differing perspectives, tried to influence the direction of Government policy in the area of inclusion. With a colleague or friend, think about the kind of power that these different groups have – you might think about the voting power of large groups of people, such as parents or disabled people, or the potential power to disrupt held by teachers' unions. From a Government perspective, what kinds of power do you think would be most persuasive? What kinds of power would be most easily resisted?

The Government was clearly influenced by the power of the teachers' unions, who expressed strong views on the inclusion of pupils who they felt to be disruptive. The teachers' agenda was reinforced by some sections of the press. Large numbers of parents supported the continuation of special schools: during previous periods of consultation, the Government had been lobbied by parents anxious to preserve special schools. At the same time, the moral imperative of the adult disability movement, campaigning for inclusion, was strong. The result, in the end, might be seen by some as compromise, by others as 'sell out'.

· · · · · · · · · · · · · · · · · · · ·

3 Activism for inclusion: a question of power

In this section we look at how some groups of people who have been seen as relatively 'powerless' have claimed power through their activism and through their challenge to existing systems. 'Activism for inclusion' has its roots in the adult disability movement. The extracts in Section 2 from Stewart Brandon's *The Invisible Wall: Niki's fight to be included* showed how much the adult disability movement influenced the tactics employed by the activists supporting the Crane family. The sit-in outside County Hall in Preston, the occupation of the building and the subsequent refusal to pay fines were all tactics that had originated in civil rights campaigns and had been taken up by adult disability activists. They had now become part of the struggle for inclusion, although in this case used not by disabled people but by their allies.

The Cranes' inclusion campaign was also directly supported by members of the adult disability movement. When Joe Whittaker appeared before the Magistrate's Court:

> A big crowd turned up to support the protest. The road to the court was blocked with supporters from the Manchester Coalition, a vociferous group who supported the rights of the disabled, across the country ...
>
> I arrived late [at the court] ... and found the protesters already inside, wheel chairs having been lugged over steps and then up by lift to the upper courts.
>
> *(Brandon, 1997, p. 62)*

A march on County Hall organized by John Kenworthy and Joe Whittaker was led by Martin Yates, a well-respected disabled rights campaigner. The transformation of young peoples' experiences to make them participants in their own education has to some extent grown out of the work of individuals and groups of adult campaigners.

Disability arts

The disability arts movement represents another way in which disabled adults and young people have sought to challenge discriminatory attitudes and practices. As Julie Allan explains:

Disabled people involved in the production of disability arts use their own bodies as weapons to subvert and undermine disabling barriers and name able bodied people as part of the problem.

(Allan, 2004)

This works on a number of different levels. Perhaps in most straightforward terms disability arts 'provides a context in which disabled people can get together, enjoy themselves and think in some way about issues of common concern' (Vasey, 1992, p. 11). There is an agenda for change too, with The National Disability Arts Forum, for example, working to promote awareness of disability issues across the arts world and in public consciousness. On a 'deeper' level, though, the arts offer a way of participants 'identifying as a disabled person' and identifying with disability culture (Vasey, 1992, p. 11).

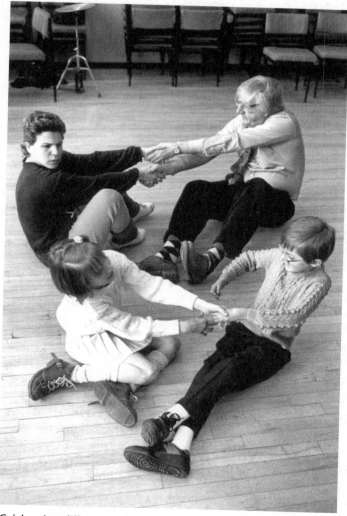

Celebrating difference.

Carousel Theatre company, Brighton: challenging perceptions about what art is and who can create it.

Importantly, performing in some way enables disabled people to be visible and to be heard, not just as individuals but as disabled individuals and groups (Allan, 2004). Claire Collinson is conscious of this in her photographs of women with ME:

> They have been given a chance to make visual an illness that is usually met with a response 'but you don't look ill', and have been empowering in the validating of my experience of an illness that some question the very existence of.
>
> *(Kelly, 1992)*

Similarly, artist Millee Hill reflects:

> I know that the time has come for me to begin to make my small contribution to that endeavour [progressing the politics of disability and the disability movement]. To acknowledge that disabled people are 'beautiful' and that paintings of them are beautiful too.
>
> *(Hill, 1992)*

The arts provide a direct way of celebrating difference and actually demonstrating pride in difference in order to make a difference. As Jane Pick (1992) has argued, 'art is a powerful propaganda tool' which disabled people need 'to promote our own positive imagery'. This can be uncomfortable for able-bodied people who are more used to taking for granted normalizing discourses and images than to having them exposed in a deliberately raw fashion.

Speaking up for yourself

Young disabled people have used techniques learned from adult disabled role models to put the case for inclusion and to claim power for themselves. Young and Powerful, a group of disabled young people, and their allies used direct action methods in their efforts to secure a mainstream placement for one of their peers:

> When we arrived at County Hall we were led straight into a big room. The Director of Education was very stern and didn't seem to listen much. He said he didn't have the power to change things without an investigation. So we agreed to meet again in a month.
>
> The evening after our meeting we were on the radio five times, there were two pieces on TV news and we made the front page of the *Nottingham Post* too!
>
> *(Comic Relief, 2001, p. 7)*

Young and Powerful focused not only on direct action but also on education and awareness raising, through conferences and through publications. Their 1993 conference focused directly on the power relationship between young people and their parents:

> Young people want parents to listen to what they have to say. Parents may have to give up their power over their children and trust young people to be in control of their own lives. Looking at what needs to happen to make this a reality is what the conference was all about.
>
> *(Paige-Smith with Etherington, 1993)*

Young and Powerful protest at County Hall, Nottingham. Photograph from the Nottingham Evening Post.

Young people talked about their relationship with their parents:

> Nigel from People First spoke about the time he came
> home late from a friend's house one night and his mom
> had called the police and registered him as a missing
> person. The police were out looking for him that night,
> yet for most people they wait 24 hours before they search.
> He was 2 hours late. At the time he felt angry but didn't
> have the language to say 'this is not the way you should
> treat me'. His parents couldn't understand why he wanted
> to leave home and live in London but he hasn't regretted
> the move he made.
>
> *(Paige-Smith with Etherington, 1993)*

The conference was organized by People First, the national self-
advocacy movement for people with learning difficulties. It stressed
the importance of role models who themselves have learning
difficulties. Nigel summed up this aspect of the conference:

> When I was 13 I realised I was going to spend my life as a
> disabled person. Because I saw no people with disabilities
> I thought that they died as children or else became able
> bodied. I needed a good role model, a light at the end of
> the tunnel. People First and the movement are my light in
> the tunnel, so many people are different and it is OK to be
> different.
>
> *(Paige-Smith with Etherington, 1993)*

Research funded by the Joseph Rowntree Foundation has also
underlined the powerful role of peer support in the lives of young
disabled people of minority ethnic heritage (Bignall *et al.*, 2002). The
young people in the study not only gave each other emotional and
social support through their peer support groups but also, for some,
were able to explore their ethnicity in a way that was not often open
to them. They could find answers about their religion or discuss issues
such as discrimination. For young deaf people especially, attending
their group gave them an opportunity to discuss religious and
ethnicity issues: this could be difficult for those whose parents used
spoken Asian languages while the young people used British Sign
Language or English. One young woman explained:

> My mother and father, they don't know sign language,
> they can't teach me about my own religion and my own
> culture.
>
> *(Bignall* et al.*, 2002)*

Intrinsic to the work of Young and Powerful was an awareness that the
location of power must move, so that different agendas are set and
different perspectives valued. Next we look at the work of one adult
disabled activist, whose work with young people has focused on this
shift of power.

Simone Aspis was sent to a special school as a child. Her responses to her schooling led her to 'speak up' about her experiences:

> As a teenager I wrote to the Secretary of State for Education Sir Keith Joseph asking if he would get me out of the special school for children with learning difficulties/SEN.
>
> Whilst doing 'time' in a boarding school I with another friend had started up the Dump Pupils with the aim of looking at the issues of being sent to a special school.
>
> *(Aspis, 2000, p. 80)*

As an adult, Simone Aspis's work has focused not only on enabling young people to 'speak up', but also on campaigning for legal recognition of young people's views within existing education systems. Simone Aspis sees young disabled people as central to the legal processes that concern them, but currently marginalized in legal terms. She has campaigned for amendments to the law that would give young people the right to take part directly in legal proceedings related to their education:

> I believe children must have the right to attend and initiate proceedings at the Special Educational Needs Tribunal in their own names. It is the child, not the parents, who has to suffer from inappropriate or poor schooling.
>
> *(Aspis, 1998, p. 9)*

She asked supporters to urge their MPs to sign up Early Day Motion (EDM) 722, that stated:

> That this House welcomes the Government's initiative towards inclusive education: calls for the 1996 Education Act and SEN Tribunal Regulations 1995 to be amended so that children have the right to initiate and attend the SEN Tribunal proceedings in their own name: and calls for the SEN Tribunal proceedings to be made more accessible so that disabled children, including those with learning difficulties, are able, with independent support, to prepare and present their own cases for their preferred schooling and support being offered to them, thus bringing children's rights in line with the United Nations Convention on the Rights of the Child and the Children Act 1989.
>
> *(Aspis, 1998, p. 9)*

Simone Aspis wants young disabled people to be actively directing the course of their own education, describing them as 'leaders' and their supporters as 'followers' (Aspis, 2000, p. 21). She gives examples of young people who have been actively involved in campaigns and decision-making processes, and shows what form that involvement might take:

> The children have shown there are many different ways that they can speak up during campaign work on inclusive education. Some children like meeting face to face with MPs, Government Ministers, Councillors and Education Officers whilst others prefer to write to them ...
>
> Not everyone likes direct action. However, there is always a role for children by simply refusing to attend a special school against their wishes. They can also speak up without even having to leave their home ... Speaking up by using the young person's own words can include sign language interpretation, maketon, and voice-over by a friend or via computers and by body language.
>
> *(Aspis, 2000, p. 33)*

Simone Aspis explores the idea of 'supported leadership', pointing out that:

> When other people become involved in supporting disabled children it is important that they never lose sight of whom they are following and where the direction must come from.
>
> *(Aspis, 2000, p. 52)*

 # Activity 15.4   Resisting change

When Simone Aspis was writing about EDM 722, only 28 MPs had signed up for it. Why do you think it had such limited support?

Imagine you are an MP who has not, as yet, signed up. Think about why you have not signed, then draft a short statement to your constituents explaining your position.

 You may not have signed up simply because the idea of disabled children actively putting their own views is new to you. You may be more familiar with the medical or charity discourses, where children with disabilities are seen as being in need of protection or cure, rather than as active agents in their own lives. You may not be aware of the different ways that disabled young people might express their views – through drawings, photographs, observations, communication aids or signing. You may feel it is too time-consuming to try to access their views in this way.

You may feel uncomfortable with the idea of young disabled people having 'power', on an equal level with professionals and parents. Simone Aspis's views challenge many stereotypes and assumptions:

The measurement of our success must not be on how well we are able to adapt (with appropriate support/ equipment) to fit into this world. Our yard-stick must be how much we are able to change the world so that everyone including Disabled People is able to determine their own lifestyles, and to be supported to live the lives we want.

(*Aspis, 2002*)

Allowing others to lead while you become a 'follower', would, for many people, require a radical readjustment of perspective, particularly if the 'leader' was young and disabled.

The 'parental lobby'

In this sub-section we look at the way that groups of adults, in particular parents, have worked towards greater inclusion and have responded to the re-definition of ideas of leadership and power set out by the adult disability movement and by activists such as Simone Aspis. This agenda is a challenging one and not all groups are either aware of it or have responded to it. You may want to think as you read about whether, in your view, this lack of response makes these groups less useful to the young people they support.

Carol Vincent and Sally Tomlinson have pointed out that 'voluntary networks and support groups organising around special education' have for some time been part of the education landscape. Such parents take a more active role than many other parents and 'produce newsletters, arrange meetings and perhaps offer an informal telephone advice service' (Vincent and Tomlinson, 1997, p. 370). These groups have been unusual, in a context that, generally speaking, has seen parents as relatively passive.

They provide forums for collective participation and action by parents, a channel for their collective voice(s).

(*Vincent and Tomlinson, 1997, p. 371*)

While commenting that it has been difficult to assess the impact of such groups, Carol Vincent and Sally Tomlinson note that some groups have managed to influence the development of LEA policy. They have also, they argue, had an impact on the way that schools and governing bodies feel about different disabilities and learning difficulties.

The impact of these groups on inclusion is difficult to assess. As Vincent and Tomlinson point out, parent groups often work locally and without publicity and they often close when money runs out. Many such groups are disability-specific and firmly rooted in the medical model of disability, so that they are perhaps more likely to focus on obtaining resources than on broader issues of the ways schools are organized.

Jenny Corbett and Brahm Norwich have pointed out that, when parents become more active, sometimes this works against inclusive ways of thinking. Parents feel they are competing for scarce resources and become 'adept at exploiting the possibilities for privileged services ... using a special needs diagnosis to improve the quality of their children's schooling' (Corbett and Norwich, 1997, pp. 379–80).

The medical model can thus become a way of drawing down resources and can work against an inclusive view of provision. Corbett and Norwich cite the case of one particular child:

> When one disruptive 10 year-old boy was to be given one-to-one tuition at an estimated cost of £14,000 a year, in order to keep him in his primary school, the *Daily Mail* reported that there was a 'mothers' revolt', as they printed a photograph of mothers taking their children out of school for the day as a protest against this boy's inclusion.
>
> *(Corbett and Norwich, 1997, p. 385)*

Alice Paige-Smith has traced the development of 'the parental lobby' and the involvement of parent-led voluntary groups in pressing for greater inclusion (Paige-Smith, 1997). One of the first groups to be established was Network 81, set up by Elizabeth and David Arrondelle. Their daughter Kirsty was going through primary school at the time that the 1981 Education Act introduced statementing. The Arrondelles found the statementing process so challenging that they set up a group to support others in the same position. By 1996:

> Network 81 had 500 members and 67 local parent pressure groups affiliated to them ... Fifty-five trained advocacy befrienders provide individual help nationally to parents.
>
> *(Paige-Smith, 1997, p. 49)*

The Arrondelles' first aim, in setting up Network 81, was to enable parents to secure the resources that would support their children effectively in mainstream education.

> While the group does not campaign by 'waving banners' according to the national co-ordinator, the group encourages parents to go out and question how LEAs respond to their requests for the provision they want for their child. The group believes 'very much in inclusive education' and sets out to 'empower parents as to how to go about getting it in mainstream schools' according to the co-ordinator. The group does also try to help parents whose children are in special schools, who may feel that they have been 'let down' by mainstream schools.
>
> *(Paige-Smith, 1997, p. 49)*

Network 81's website shows that their focus is on giving information, either directly to parents through their advice lines, or as part of LEA training. They aim for empowerment of parent users of services, through giving information.

Parents in Partnership, in contrast, when describing their activities to Alice Paige-Smith, saw themselves as a campaigning 'lobby group', with a position firmly rooted in the social model of disability and in a rights-based perspective. The London-based group was formed in 1984 and later changed its name to Parents for Inclusion (Pi). Although Pi still offers advice and support to individual parents, it is concerned with campaigning and awareness raising on a broader scale. In particular, Pi has focused on including Black and minority ethnic parents in its work.

Pi aims:

> To bring about social change by providing effective advice, information and training that enables parents and disabled people of all ages not only to be included, but also to be empowered to become leaders in this change.
>
> *(Parents for Inclusion, 2000, p. 2)*

In this, it echoes some of the points made by Simone Aspis and uses the idea of leadership that we looked at earlier. In addition, Pi has allied itself with the Alliance for Inclusive Education (ALLFIE), a campaigning group led by disabled people, and with Disability Equality in Education (DEE), a training and awareness-raising organization also led by disabled people.

Jan Nicholas, then chief executive of Pi, spoke about the centrality of young people's experiences to what Pi does.

> Being allies means seeking to support and empower our young people to become self advocating. And we probably should do more to create opportunities to listen to them and to hear what is important to them. Hence we value the advice of Disabled Adults – who after all know the oppression that is felt by disabled children better than anyone simply because they were children once. It means we can keep the disabled child's perspective central to our work at Pi and our thinking.
>
> *(Nicholas quoted in Aspis, 2000, p. 58)*

For some of the larger, more established voluntary organizations, such a shift has taken longer and involved a challenge to received ways of working.

4 Who sets the agenda?

For the disabled: *of* the disabled

Mike Oliver has distinguished between 'organisations for the disabled and organisations of disabled people' (Oliver, 1990, p. 113). The difference, he argues, lies in who controls and runs the organization: for an organization to be 'of disabled people', he argues, 'at least 50 per cent of the management committee or controlling body must, themselves, be disabled' (Oliver, 1990, p. 113). Oliver describes organizations run by non-disabled people as fundamentally taking a 'charitable' view of the people they work for, assuming that they cannot take control of their own lives and creating dependency. In addition, he sees the people who run these organizations as operating within a medical, rather than a social model of disability. Quite quickly, he argues, such people get 'out of touch', becoming part of the existing establishment and eventually focusing on their own interests.

Although we could argue that this can, and does, happen to those involved in the other group as well, arguments such as those put forward by Mike Oliver, alongside the models of self-advocacy and leadership advanced by Simone Aspis, have led to what Olga Miller has described as 'much soul-searching' within disability-focused charities (Miller, 2000, p. 246). While we return to the role of the larger voluntary organizations in bringing about change, here we look at the way that a smaller organization, the Down's Syndrome Association (DSA), has moved towards a more radical agenda.

◯ Activity 15.5   Shifts in power

Now read Chapter 7, Reader 1, 'Inclusion – looking forward' by Carol Boys.

As you read, note down examples of any 'shifts in power' that you see in Carol Boys's account. Look at her experience as a parent, at her son Alex's experiences and at the way the DSA has changed.

Alex was born at about the time that parents of disabled children were first given rights in law about where and how their children were educated. Carol took an active part in his school life and on occasion took control of his classroom experiences. She chose where he went to secondary school – clearly Alex was not totally happy with that choice. We see here that power had shifted, but to parents rather than to young people themselves. Even with that shift in power, Carol was not able to find a mainstream place that seemed right for Alex.

Within the DSA, power is gradually moving towards users of services, rather than providers. Carol, the DSA's chief executive, is a parent with direct experience of disability, not a 'career' worker in the voluntary sector. The DSA now has trustees with Down syndrome and is producing materials directly for people with Down syndrome, rather than for their parents or carers.

There is some evidence in Carol Boys's account that the gradual shift in power in the DSA, in particular the solidarity that the Down to Earth group found in each other's company, has taken some of its workers by surprise. She lists some of the activities that people with Down's syndrome 'could' do. The Down to Earth group is, in Mike Oliver's terms, an 'organization of' people with Down syndrome, but Carol Boys does not suggest that the DSA itself is planning to move in that direction. She does, though, look forward to a time when representation of people with Down syndrome within the organization will be greater.

We see that the Down to Earth group has challenged some of the traditional views held in the DSA: as a result, the organization has changed its position. The *Down to Earth* magazine, for example, is moving from 'human interest' stories to articles on issues affecting people with Down syndrome. The DSA has had to consider who its audience is and what position it should take when, for example, parents and young people do not share the same views.

The chapter shows the DSA in a state of change, with the views of its members with Down syndrome having an increasing impact on how it works and what it says. It is possible that in the future the DSA will need to consider whether it is an organization 'of' or 'for' people with Down syndrome. Will Down to Earth become a separate organization?

Puppet or partner?

As Olga Miller has pointed out, it can be misleading to think about 'the voluntary sector' as a whole, because of its sheer size and diversity. She estimates that there are over 40,000 organizations in the UK, not counting many small local initiatives (Miller, 2000, p. 243). She records how disability rights activists have been critical of the sector as 'an anachronism, embedded within its Victorian philanthropic roots' (Miller, 2000, p. 242) and quotes Mike Oliver's views on the voluntary sector:

> The continued presence and influence of ... traditional organizations is now positively harmful both in terms of the images they promote and the scarce resources they use up. The time has now come for them to get out of the way. Disabled people and other minority groups are now

empowering themselves and this process could be far
more effective without the dead hand of a hundred years
of charity weighing them down.

(Oliver cited in Miller, 2000, pp. 250–1)

Particular targets for disability rights activists have been fund-raising
telethons that present disabled people as objects of pity: the website
www.stoppity.org reflects the campaign in the USA against Jerry
Lewis's national fund-raising telethon. In the UK there have been
major concerns about whether the voluntary sector relates to the
Government as either 'partner or puppet'. Many of the larger charities
actively work with Government agencies on service delivery: they run
homes or schools, for example. To some it appears that they have
become agents of Government policy. Andrea Kelmanson, former
director of the National Centre for Volunteering, expressed concerns
that charities receiving Government money were being expected to
carry out the politicians' agenda:

> I understand that who pays the piper calls the tune, but
> funders have a responsibility that just because they've got
> the money doesn't mean they've got all the answers.
> They're missing opportunities if they don't talk to those
> receiving funds.

(Kelmanson quoted in McCurry, 2001)

Camilla Batmanghelidjl, founder of the south London charity Kids
Company, said she was worried that sometimes, when the charity had
been consulted by the Government on spending on children's services,
the agenda had already been set. In her view:

> We take part in discussions but there are one or two
> people who have already decided what and how the
> money will be spent and the rest of us tag along.

(Batmanghelidj quoted in McCurry, 2001)

Social solidarity for some?

If the agenda has already been set, as in Camilla Batmanghelidjl's
experience it has, who has set it? Olga Miller suggests that, though
there have been many benefits arising out of the disability
movement's challenges to the voluntary sector 'establishment', there
have also been losses. In particular, there has been the loss, she says,
of the 'greater awareness of what social solidarity might mean to
other groups marginalized by society but with little or no organized
support within the voluntary sector' (Miller, 2000, p. 247). Those with
'non-disability' difficulties and with no 'organized support', for
example, young people with moderate learning difficulties or
emotional and behavioural disorders, are likely to belong to ethnic
minorities or other sectors generally considered disadvantaged. As
small groups of parents organize themselves into lobby groups around

existing or 'newly discovered' disabilities such as attention deficit disorder, the marginalization of other disadvantaged groups grows:

> Well informed and articulate, such parents exhibit skill in mobilizing pressure groups in order to lobby for change. These parents are usually white and middle class.
>
> *(Miller, 2000, p. 248)*

No such 'social solidarity' exists for pupils with challenging behaviour or moderate learning difficulties. Alan Dyson has made a similar point, suggesting that one of the results achieved by the 'highly politicized and articulate disability movement' has been to focus debates on disability (Dyson, 1997, p. 155). This focus is, he argues, evident within the inclusion movement:

> [T]he concern to which the inclusion movement appears invariably to return is the right of *disabled* children to be placed in mainstream schools; an important issue, to be sure, but not one that is immediately relevant to the wide range of children experiencing educational difficulties who are *already* placed in the mainstream.
>
> *(Dyson, 1997, p. 155)*

Alan Dyson, while not wishing to underestimate the importance of disability issues in education, argues that perspectives should be wider. Many problems seen in the education system, he suggests, such as disaffection, low attainment, underachievement and disruption, are 'connected to patterns of disadvantage and inequality in society as a whole':

> [I]t seems to me to be undeniable that poverty, unemployment, lack of opportunity, poor health and health care, criminality and a whole range of other sources of stress on families and children are reflected in the difficulties which those children bring to, and present in, their schools. They are, in other words, difficulties *in* education but not, primarily, difficulties *of* education.
>
> *(Dyson, 1997, p. 155)*

You will have noticed that much of this unit has been concerned with disabled children, their rights in law, the organizations that support them, the role of their parents and their aspirations to social change. In the next section we look at the impact that this focus has had on groups who are marginalized for other reasons.

5 Social disadvantage: the 'out groups'

An unpopular cause

Camilla Batmanghelidjl, who found herself 'tagging along' in discussions with the Government, is the director of Kids Company, an organization that focuses on 'the others'. Set up in 1996, Kids Company was originally based in six railway arches in Camberwell, south London, and so became known as 'the Arches'. According to its website (www.kidsco.org.uk) the young people it serves live in 'severely challenging inner city environments' and have 'slipped through the net of statutory services'. Many have been excluded from statutory services because of their behaviour. A Youth Service report in 2000 concluded that the young people using the Arches 'come from a particularly disadvantaged population group with a high level of deprivation, abuse, specific learning difficulties, mental health problems and drug abuse' (Kids Company, 2003a).

When the National Children's Bureau evaluated the work of Kids Company in 2001 (Kids Company, 2003a), it found that:

- 57 per cent of the young people did not live in their family home;
- 58 per cent were Black;
- 41 per cent had experienced mainstream education in negative ways;
- 23 per cent had been permanently excluded;
- 32 per cent had been arrested by the police prior to their engagement with Kids Company.

All the young people interviewed in the evaluation believed that the Arches project had made a positive difference in their lives, in terms of behaviour and attitude, educational improvement, communication skills, confidence and self-esteem. Children reported:

> It is somewhere I can get away from my house, make new friends and stay out of crime.
>
> *(Alfie, 14, Kids Company, 2003b)*

> Brilliant, I have my own special staff, we sit and talk every week.
>
> *(Luke, 12, Kids Company, 2003b)*

The Crime Concern Evaluation, carried out in 2002, described Kids Company as:

> a model of much of what government is attempting to achieve in its policies to tackle social exclusion.

It is a real example of a community-based, needs-led,
'joined up' project, with a rare ability to reach out to large
numbers of profoundly disadvantaged young people.

(Kids Company, 2003a)

Kids Company is an example of a small-scale voluntary organization
operating outside the 'disability' model and with a group with a poor
public image. That group, those with 'severely challenging behaviour'
was the one, you will recall, to whom Baroness Blackstone specifically
referred during the debate on Section 316, describing them as a group
for whom mainstream placement was 'not appropriate'.

Although Kids Company has been high-profile and has enjoyed the
support of royalty and politicians, it has experienced difficulties with
local planners and residents. In April 2003, *The Guardian* reported:

> At the end of a tortuous week, Camilla Batmanghelidjh
> padlocked the gate of Kids Company, the renowned
> youth charity for wayward children ...

> As of today, the charity is under orders to leave its
> premises under railway arches in Camberwell, south
> London, because the local council and the courts have
> decided it was an inappropriate planning use for the
> building. But Kids Company says it won't leave, not least
> because it has nowhere else to go ...

> [A] vociferous group of neighbours and some local
> politicians believe it attracts young men bent on crime
> and antisocial behaviour. Though Kids Company has
> pleaded for more time, saying it may have found
> alternative premises to move into in August, the residents
> and council say the die is cast. If Kids Company returns to
> the building on Monday, Southwark council will begin
> legal proceedings ...

> Reflecting on her situation with youngsters who rely on
> Kids Company for education, counselling and sometimes,
> parenting, Ms Batmanghelidjh is bitter. 'There is all this
> talk about planning and politics, but who is talking about
> the children. The people against us are determined and
> articulate and they have councillors on their side. The
> children don't seem to matter because they don't vote
> and neither do their parents. If people are really serious
> about dealing with social exclusion, they can't allow work
> like this to be devastated by petty local politics.'

(Muir, 2003)

☼ Activity 15.6   NIMBY?

The Guardian article quoted above reported the secretary of the local tenants' association as saying:

> We are not campaigning against Camilla. We fully support what she does. It is wonderful work. Who else would want to do it? But it is the wrong work for this area.
>
> *(Muir, 2003)*

Working with a colleague or friend, imagine that one of you is a young person who uses the Kids Company centre and the other is a member of the tenants' association. Role play your discussion about the future of the centre.

Allies and advocates

Olga Miller pointed out that some groups of marginalized young people and their families are outside existing networks of 'support groups' and pressure groups. Camilla Batmanghelidjh acknowledges this fact when she refers to the powerlessness of the young people using the Arches. The users of the Arches are unlikely, at this point at least, to be able to resist the local agenda on their own, without allies from the 'outside world' or legal representation. Those who join in as allies are not likely to win friends. Alan Yentob, the BBC's director of drama and a Kids Company trustee, along with all the other trustees, was warned that he would face legal action and a claim for 'substantial damages' if the charity did not move out (Muir, 2003).

Other workers with unpopular causes have found themselves in similar circumstances. We saw in Unit 1 how the Communities Empowerment Network (CEN), which represents excluded pupils at exclusion appeals, was vilified nationally when it represented two boys who had made death threats to a teacher.

CEN's director, Gerry German, has written about his organization's view on the exclusion of Black pupils from school (German, 2001). CEN is concerned that Black African-Caribbean pupils are four to six times more likely to be excluded from school than their white and Asian counterparts. It asks questions about the context of exclusions, such as:

- how many Black governors and teachers are there?

- what about admissions policies and enrolment/selection?

- how are opportunities rationed through streaming, setting and tiering?

- what about relevance and positive images in curriculum content, textbooks and other resources?

(German, 2001, p. 4)

In addition, it makes recommendations about the conduct of exclusion hearings, for example, that:

- adjudicating bodies should have at least one person from the same ethnic group as the excluded pupil

- every adjudicator [should] be trained in the DfES guidance and in equal opportunities, anti-racist strategies.

(German, 2001, pp. 3–4)

However, despite its awareness of the context of exclusion, CEN's most pressing concern is that individual excluded pupils be effectively represented:

School exclusions are more likely to be successfully resisted when pupils and their families are represented by independent experienced advocates who understand the system and the workings of racism.

(German, 2001, p. 2)

Good representation is, in the end, a more active concern than good practice guides or awareness raising.

Activity 15.7   Ways of resisting

Young and Powerful 'resisted exclusion' in a way very different from that put forward by Gerry German of CEN. How do you think Young and Powerful's approach of sit-ins and direct action would be viewed if adopted by the young people CEN represents?

Gerry German and CEN are anxious that the views of parents and young people are represented:

We ... emphasise the fact that we operate only in partnership with them: we don't work *for* them, only *with* them. We intervene only with their full approval, and we are careful to ensure that the young people are willing for us to work with them and represent them.

(German, 2001, p. 2)

CEN is offering a dedicated service:

> When we are approached by parents, we tell them how we
> operate: first, we believe their children, and second, we
> provide 100% support.

> *(German, 2001, p. 2)*

But in this case the challenge to exclusion does not come via what
Olga Miller (2000, p. 248) called 'social solidarity' because, for many
of the pupils affected by exclusion, there is no social solidarity to draw
on. The pupils come from groups that are marginalized and lacking
in power, in Gus John's words, 'the out group' (John, 2002, p. 7).
Instead, the challenge comes directly through advocacy, offered by a
person trained and experienced in exclusion law, using their
information and experience on behalf of others.

This may, however, miss the point that many groups originally
without solidarity ultimately gained it by getting together against the
odds. Disabled people found it hard to get together in the face of
disabling barriers to transport, for example, and across differences in
impairments; lesbian and gay people had to find ways of finding each
other against the pressures to be invisible. Can you imagine other 'out
groups' gaining solidarity in time? Or might it be argued that for
some people this isn't within their 'social resources', or is simply not
supported by the current culture? Maybe all that young people with
'(social) emotional and behavioural difficulties' have in common is
the experience of being labelled, but, then, this may have
consequences enough to lead them into finding solidarity with each
other. These questions, which represent genuine pondering on the part
of the course team, are important for any discussion of who brings
about change for young people who currently lack power.

Information and advice

A number of both disability-related and broader-based voluntary
organizations work to provide information that can enable users of
services, often parents, to take a more active part in the processes
affecting their children's education. The Independent Panel for Special
Education Advice (IPSEA) gives free and independent advice to
parents, usually by way of its free telephone service. It has deliberately
focused its advice work on low-income families.

> A recent study by Strathclyde University found that
> children from better-off families get special education
> help more easily. They are not necessarily the people in
> greatest need. In fact, the people in greatest need often
> have the double problem of disability and low social
> status. IPSEA's casework bears out this view. We believe it
> is essential that we provide a comprehensive service to

meet the needs of those parents most in need of support. If their children do not receive the educational provision their needs call for, they risk being further disadvantaged for life.

(IPSEA, 2003)

IPSEA's website records that 50 per cent of calls to the organization's advice lines come from households with an overall income of below £15,000 a year, while 27 per cent of callers have incomes of less than £10,000 a year.

Similarly, the Advisory Centre for Education (ACE) has targeted potentially marginalized families through its work on advice lines, publications and web-based materials. Its Education Step-by-Step project aims to train and support advice workers in local organizations that work with disadvantaged, minority ethnic and refugee parents. In 2002, over 41,000 of ACE's advice booklets, covering bullying, exclusion, special educational needs and disability discrimination, were downloaded from their website (www.ace-ed.org.uk). The first four months of 2003 recorded 21,000 downloads, nearly 2,000 of which were the ACE booklet on race discrimination.

Image used at exclusion conference, Outside Looking In, organized by the Children's Society and ACE.

ACE's work on exclusion includes not only a designated advice line and written materials for parents but campaigning work based on data gathered from parents who contact the advice lines. Like CEN, ACE has argued that excluded pupils need trained advocates. ACE has gone further to argue for the extension of legal representation for parents at exclusion appeals and fairer appeal procedures, including legally qualified chairpersons (ACE, 2002, p. 13).

Young Minds, a national charity focusing on children's mental health, has, like ACE and IPSEA, a range of information-giving services. As well as a parent helpline, it has publications and training materials designed to inform and raise awareness. Its website (www.youngminds.org.uk) provides a range of information, for use by professionals, parents and young people themselves, as well as publications it has developed for campaigning purposes.

These smaller voluntary organizations are often at what Olga Miller (2000, p. 242) has called 'the cutting edge of contemporary service provision', seeing the immediate impact of new policies and working to change values and perceptions, often in 'unpopular' areas. However, because they take a principled position on controversial issues, they can find themselves in difficulties. When ACE, for example, sponsored a conference that looked at the experiences of excluded children and their families, *The Guardian*, which had written sympathetically about the conference, published a number of angry letters accusing ACE of condoning the impact on other pupils of bad behaviour.

Many small charities depend on sources of funding that are vulnerable to outside pressure. We have already looked at the vilification of Gerry German at CEN. Perhaps more significant than the vilification was the media attack on the Lottery funding that supported CEN. Gus John, CEN's chair, launched an angry counter-attack:

> The *Daily Mail* appears to have a massive problem with principles of equity and justice. It appears to want to establish 'in groups' and 'out groups' as far as the recipients of lottery funding are concerned. It says nothing, however, about the fact that those relegated to the confines of the 'out group' are amongst the biggest spenders on lottery tickets.
>
> As a collective group across the country, should the parents of students excluded or belonging to communities suffering disproportionate numbers of exclusions be debarred from buying lottery tickets, or should they just not be eligible to benefit from lottery handouts?
>
> *(John, 2002, p. 7)*

The voluntary sector as a whole is traditionally beset by funding problems: small charities taking unpopular positions in relation to marginalized young people can find themselves particularly vulnerable to financial crises.

The Joseph Rowntree Foundation has supported research into the experiences of voluntary and community organizations led by Black and minority ethnic people (McLeod *et al.*, 2001). The results of the study challenged the perception that these organizations are usually small, informal bodies: over 90 per cent had a formal legal status and just over half had an annual income of over £50,000. However, the organizations surveyed were apprehensive about their sustainability, particularly in connection with a lack of access to core funding activities and lack of official recognition. Their concerns echoed those of Camilla Batmanghelidjh, in that they were worried about their exclusion from the partnerships and alliances that now form the basis of much bidding for funds.

Activity 15.8   Campaigning for change

Imagine you are trying to raise money to support an advice-giving service for disaffected young people who have been excluded from school. In the course of your organization's advice giving you have made formal complaints about exclusion practices in local schools and about the LEA's own processes. Think about the sort of campaign you would run. Who would you target for money? What choices might you have to face?

You would possibly need to overcome quite a lot of hostility and prejudice in relation to the young people you work with. You might want to focus on success stories and approach funding organizations with a history of working with marginalized groups. However, you might think about the implications of accepting money from statutory bodies. Would this make you less able to be outspoken?

6   Conclusion: where the light is

We have seen that change is brought about by many different forces. Sometimes it arises out of persuasion, the winning of hearts and minds through argument and information. Sometimes it happens more directly, through legal intervention on behalf of an individual or through a focused campaign. Often change is patchy and too slow: reports in the education press have suggested, for example, that at current rates some LEAs would take over a hundred years to reach the levels of inclusion now operating in the London Borough of Newham (Gold, 2003).

Mark Vaughan, founder of CSIE, spoke robustly about the DfES's failure to intervene:

> Every time we have written to them asking what they are
> going to do about the discrepancy between authorities
> they just dismiss it with bland bureaucratic language
> about local freedom to interpret the law.
>
> *(Vaughan quoted in Gold, 2003, p. 19)*

Mark Vaughan's exasperated tone is understandable: CSIE hoped to
persuade others of the moral imperative of its position. CSIE's website
reflects the range of its activities, which include prolific publications,
data collection, information packs and position papers, as well as
events celebrating inclusive practice. It has drawn up an Inclusion
Charter and publicized good practice, in particular 'the Newham
story', which, you will recall, we discussed in Units 1 and 10.

And yet, after twenty years of campaigning at CSIE, Mark Vaughan
reflects that, in his view, CSIE's goal of 'a fully de-segregated education
system' will not be achieved in his lifetime:

> I have observed a fundamental conservatism in British
> education, in spite of some inspirational changes. The
> investments in a dual, segregated system are old and run
> deep in our society, and British people – sadly – do not
> warm to the idea of seeing inclusion as the basic human
> rights issue it is.
>
> *(Vaughan, 2002, p. 46)*

Noam Chomsky, linguist, writer and political activist, told the
following story:

> There's a famous joke about a drunk under a lamppost
> looking at the ground and somebody comes up and asks
> him 'What are you looking for?' He says, 'I'm looking for
> a pencil that I dropped'. They said, 'Well, where did you
> drop it?' He says, 'Oh, I dropped it across the street'. 'Well,
> why are you looking here?' 'This is where the light is.'
>
> *(Chomsky quoted in Kreisler, 2002)*

If you look back through this unit, and through the course as a whole,
at 'where the light is', where would you find it?

It might be in the commitment of individuals whose personal
contribution we have looked at in this unit, people who have made a
stand or worked, often for free, for changes in the law. Or it might be
in the work of those unnamed people who, as Chomsky acknowledged
in his own area of activism, 'work on it' on a daily basis.

> Working on it day after day, all the time, that's hard, and
> that's important, and that's what changes the world.
>
> *(Chomsky quoted in Kreisler, 2002)*

It might be in the work of the young people who have become
involved in the campaigns we have looked at, for example, the young
people who supported Niki Crane:

A very persuasive argument for inclusion came from Niki's friends at the primary school. A large group of eleven years olds gathered to voice their dismay at the council's decision. If Niki wasn't allowed in the school it would be 'daft' said one, while two girls explained that Niki 'Shouldn't be made to leave his friends. He knows us, knows our faces.' The friends couldn't understand what all the fuss was about. Why couldn't he go to the big school with them? What was the problem? Answers on a postcard to the Chief Education Officer.

(Brandon, 1997, p. 56)

Or young people like those who challenged bullying and racism in their schools.

I just tried to ignore it, but I felt so trapped and alone. Then, with the help from Leeds Racial Harrassment Project, I met up with some other young people who had the same experiences and we started STAR [Stand Together Against Racism].

(Candice in Comic Relief, 2001, p. 17)

We have seen and heard racism, things like racist name calling or people telling racist jokes. Even if it is not against us directly we don't think it is right and don't want to live in a place where it happens.

(Zara and Fallon in Comic Relief, 2001, p. 17)

It may be in the alliances that have formed to bring about change – the links that supported the work of the Special Education Consortium, or the links between the adult disability movement and young people's groups such as Young and Powerful. It might be the links between campaigning organizations and higher education: Mark Vaughan (2002), for instance, writes about the early impact of The Open University on CSIE's work and on the more recent co-operation with academics Tony Booth and Mel Ainscow that led to the development of the *Index for Inclusion*. CSIE also has close contacts with the Bolton Institute, whose Inclusion Data we have drawn on throughout this course.

If we are looking for commitment to increasing the participation of potentially marginalized groups, then 'light' might be coming from the direction of the work of large charitable trusts, such as the Joseph Rowntree Foundation, which has consistently sponsored innovative research into the experiences of previously overlooked groups. You may recall from Unit 4, for example, Jenny Morris's work with young disabled people, focusing on their right to 'have a say' in their own lives. Other Rowntree-sponsored research has focused on minority ethnic families with disabled children and on experiences of exclusion in multicultural communities.

It is impossible to pick out one single area of light: the important thing is that, together, activists have worked to bring about a climate where change is possible and where it is seen to be necessary. We close with Kreisler's record of Noam Chomsky's advice to activists, whatever their area of concern:

> Join with others, and you can do a lot of things ...
>
> It's got a big multiplier effect ... The reason we don't live in a dungeon is because people joined together to change things ...
>
> Try to join with others who share your interests to learn more and to act responsively.
>
> *(Chomsky quoted in Kreisler, 2002)*

'Act responsively' (Chomsky, quoted in Kreisler, 2002).

References

Advisory Centre for Education (ACE) (2002) *Action on Exclusion: an update*, Bulletin 107.

Allan, J. (2004) 'Disability arts and the performance of ideology' in Gabel, S. (ed.) *Disability Studies in Education*, Boston, Peter Lang.

Aspis, S. (2000) *Disabled Children with Learning Difficulties Fight for Inclusive Education*, Willesden, Changing Perspectives.

Aspis, S. (2002) 'Updating the social model'. Available from http//www.bcodp.org.uk/activate/issue47/updatingsocmod.html [accessed 16 May 2002].

Bignall, T., Butt, J. and Pagarani, D. (2002) *'Something to Do': the development of peer support groups for young black and minority ethnic disabled people*, London, Policy Press.

Brandon, S. (1997) *The Invisible Wall: Niki's fight to be included*, Hesketh Bank, Parents with Attitude.

Comic Relief (2001) *The Comic Relief Guide to Changing the World, the Universe and Everything*, London, Comic Relief.

Corbett, J. and Norwich, B. (1997) 'Special needs and client rights: the changing social and political context of special educational research', *British Educational Research Journal*, 23(3), pp. 379–89.

Department for Education and Science (DfES) (2003) *The Report of the Special Schools Working Group*. Available from http://www.dfes.gov.uk/consultations2/04/DfES-SSWG%20Main%20Report.pdf [accessed 27 November 2003].

Dyson, A. (1997) 'Social and educational disadvantage: reconnecting special needs education', *British Journal of Special Education*, 24(4), pp. 152–7.

German, G. (2001) 'The need for Black advocacy in relation to school exclusions', conference paper, 'Turning children away from crime', 6 March.

Gold, K. (2003) 'Give us inclusion ... but not yet', *The Times Educational Supplement*, 23 May.

Hansard (2000) 19 December. Available from http://www.parliament.the-stationery-office.co.uk/pa/ld200001/ldhansrd/vo001219/text/01219–04.htm [accessed 12 Februry 2004)].

Hill, M. (1992) 'To paint or not to paint?', *Disability Arts Magazine*, 2(3). Available from http://www.leeds.ac.uk/disability-studies/archiveuk [accessed 29 August 2003].

Hugill, B. (1993) 'Down's teenager defies charges over school choice', *The Observer*, 14 November.

Independent Panel for Special Education Advice (IPSEA) (1994) 'Who knows best?', *Special Edition*, newsletter of IPSEA, January.

Independent Panel for Special Education Advice (IPSEA) (1997a) 'Wonderful news', *Special Edition*, newsletter of IPSEA, September.

Independent Panel for Special Education Advice (IPSEA) (1997b) 'Niki Crane – the struggle continues', *Special Edition*, newsletter of IPSEA, September.

Independent Panel for Special Education Advice (IPSEA) (2003): www.ipsea.org [accessed 29 May 2003].

Independent Panel for Special Education Advice (IPSEA) (1998) 'In my opinion', *Special Edition*, newsletter of the IPSE, July.

John, G. (2002) 'The Glyn Technology School exclusion affair and CEN', press release, Communities Empowerment Network (CEN).

Kelly, B. (1992) 'Interviews', *Disability Arts Magazine*, 2(3). Available from http://www.leeds.ac.uk/disability-studies/archiveuk [accessed 29 August 2003].

Kids Company (2003a) 'The effectiveness of Kids Company'. Available from http://www.kidsco.org.uk/collectiveresearchoutcomes.htm (accessed 29 May 2003).

Kids Company (2003b) 'What the kids say'. Available from http://www.kidsco.org.uk/kidssay.htm (accessed 29 May 2003).

Kreisler, H. (2002) 'Activism, anarchism and power: conversation with Noam Chomsky', 22 March. Available from http://globetrotter.berkeley.edu/people2/Chomsky/chomsky-con5.html [accessed 30 May 2003].

Lamb, B. (2001) 'Coded messages', *The Times Educational Supplement*, 6 July.

McCurry, P. (2001) 'Charities will lose sympathy for doing the government's work', *The Guardian*, 27 April.

McLeod, M., Owen, D. and Khamis, C. (2001) *Black and Minority Ethnic Voluntary and Community Organisations: their role and future development in England and Wales*, London, Policy Studies Institute.

Miller, O. (2000) 'Inclusion and the role of the voluntary sector' in Daniels, H. (ed.) *Special Education Re-formed: beyond rhetoric?*, London, Falmer Press.

Muir, H. (2003) 'Children's champion ready to defy the law', *The Guardian*, 26 April.

Munro, N. (2003) 'Exclusions milestone a millstone for ministers', *The Times Educational Supplement (Scotland)*, 21 February.

Oliver, M. (1990) *The Politics of Disablement*, Basingstoke, Macmillan.

Paige-Smith, A. with Etherington, A. (1993) 'Introduction', Young and Powerful conference report.

Paige–Smith, A. (1997) 'The rise and impact of the parental lobby: including voluntary groups and the education of children with learning difficulties or disabilities' in Wolfendale, S. (ed.) *Working with Parents of SEN Children after the Code of Practice*, London, David Fulton.

Parents for Inclusion (2000) *Including all Children: annual report 1999/ 2000*, London, Parents for Inclusion.

Parents for Inclusion (2003) 'Government breaks promises on inclusion for disabled children'. Available from http:// www.parentsforinclusion.org/pressrel.htm [accessed 25 November 2003].

Pick, J. (1992) 'Letters', *Disability Arts Magazine*, **2**(3). Available from http://www.leeds.ac.uk/disability-studies/archiveuk [accessed 29 August 2003].

Rieser, R. and Mason, M. (1992) *Disability Equality in the Classroom: a human rights issue*, London, Disability Equality in Education.

Simmons, K. (2000) 'Parents, legislation and inclusion' in Daniels, H. (ed.) *Special Education Re-formed: beyond rhetoric?*, London, Falmer Press.

Vasey, S. (1992) 'Disability arts and culture: an introduction to key issues and questions' in Lees, S. (ed.) *Disability Arts and Culture Papers*, London, Shape Publications.

Vaughan, M. (2002) 'A consistent campaign', *Support for Learning*, **17**(1), pp. 44–6.

Vincent, C. and Tomlinson, S. (1997) 'Home–school relationships: "the swarming of disciplinary mechanisms"?', *British Educational Research Journal*, **23**(3), pp. 361–79.

UNIT 16   Imagine better

Prepared for the course team by Kieron Sheehy and Jonathan Rix

Contents

1 Introduction

The ways in which we understand and practise inclusive education today are relatively new, and this gives us the luxury of considering where they may lead. Our future understanding and practices of inclusion may end up bearing little resemblance to current ideas. In this unit we discuss some ideas about the future of inclusive education and how technological developments and innovations may affect that future.

Predicting the future is difficult. Past predictions had it that, for example:

> 'Everything that can be invented has been invented.' Charles H. Duell, Commissioner, U.S. Office of Patents, 1899

> 'Heavier-than-air flying machines are impossible.' Lord Kelvin, President, Royal Society, 1895

> 'Computers in the future may weigh no more than 1.5 tons.' *Popular Mechanics*, forecasting the relentless march of science, 1949

> *(English Teachers Network, 2003)*

These predictions were about 'objective' technological developments. Clearly, technological changes intertwine with, and influence, changes in society and will shape any predictions we might make about the development of education. In 1971 a national competition asked teachers to describe how they thought their schools would be in the year 2000 (Lister, 1975). Educational, social and technological changes were seen as being enmeshed. Some predictions were closer to what actually happened than others.

> Our grounds include playing fields and a mixed small holding (flowers, fruit, vegetables and livestock) ...

> The emphasis on the 'list of objectives' is the greatest educational change since the seventies. Everyone has access to these and we all know where we are going ...

> The word 'teacher' is a bit dated now. Child adviser would be better ...

> Education to 15 years is free to the student. Loans are made to students to enable them to study after 15 years of age ...

> We haven't got classes anymore, everyone is free to work at his own rate and where he will ...

> The PTC [personal tutor computer] keeps a daily record of the child's academic progress, interests, and at the end of

term, the PTC evaluates *all* of the child's work and
suggests areas of difficulty and achievement ...

We have to restrict the use of hovercrafts by pupils below
the age of 12.

(Lister, 1975, pp. 14, 15, 32, 39, 46, 52, 58)

Many of the teachers' predictions involved the 'latest' technology,
such as tape recorders, televisions, computers and even the hovercraft.
These would be used to allow schools to change physically (circular
buildings, changeable or mobile buildings or dispersed or non-
existent buildings), give greater freedom and control to children in
how they learn and when they learn it, and free teachers to help their
pupils do this. However, some teachers envisaged a future of
dehumanized schools, governed by punitive transnational laws. Here,
pupils and teachers would be passive 'puppets' whose behaviour is
constantly under surveillance and recorded.

The community back us up by treating any child not
wearing an absence badge for what he is – a nuisance
wasting public money. He is refused service on public
transport, shopkeepers, places of amusement, etc. ...

It could be said that the individual is conditioned so
much that he has lost the right to be unhappy.

(Lister, 1975, pp. 93, 103)

Our stance on inclusive education is that it is based on a set of values
and we want these values to inform, underpin and shape change. It is,
therefore, this aspect of the possible future that we will be discussing,
the interaction between inclusive values and some future
developments.

Learning outcomes

By the end of this unit you will have:

- thought about how changes in the context of inclusive education
  may influence its nature;

- identified ways in which developments in technology can have an
  impact upon our social existence and identity;

- explored ways in which technological developments interact with
  discourses of human rights and inclusion;

- critically assessed predictions of the future of education with regard
  to inclusion.

Issues of imagined futures might be an area you choose to explore in
your interview for TMA 05.

Resources for this unit

As you study this unit we ask you to read the following chapters:

For Activity 16.3:

- Chapter 10 in Reader 1, 'Has classroom teaching served its day?' by Donald McIntyre.

For Activity 16.4:

- Chapter 11 in Reader 1, 'New technology and inclusion: the world (wide web) is not enough' by Kieron Sheehy.

You may also need access to an online computer as an option within Activity 16.7.

2   Shaping the schools of the future

Why bother with the future?

We begin with a belief that it is important to know the sort of future that we want for our children and grandchildren. This is important because, as Elizabeth Murphy argues:

> We cannot truly control, invent or even predict the future. However, we can hold a vision for it in order to inspire our efforts and actions. Sharing this vision with as many people as possible increases the potential that the vision will serve as a blueprint for future developments. Thus, regardless of when, or what we believe the future will be, our individual and collective visions are what matter.
>
> *(Murphy, 1996, p. 5)*

And as Richard Reiser quotes:

> Never doubt that a small group of thoughtful committed citizens can change the world: indeed it's the only thing that ever has.
>
> *(Margaret Mead, quoted in Reiser, 2001, p. 132)*

Having come this far in the course you will have developed your own ideas about inclusive education and the ways in which you would wish it to develop. The path that inclusive education takes will undoubtedly be influenced by large-scale cultural, economic and social forces that develop within society. There is evidence that we are entering a time in which these forces are undergoing profound and accelerating change.

> Setting the scene for the future ... most social theorists would agree that the kind of changes we are experiencing as we move into the 21st century are profound and may

even be as significant for us and the changes in our lives
as the replacement of feudalism by capitalism was for our
ancestors in a previous epoch. The fundamentals of this
are well known: the move from a fordist to a post-fordist
mode of production; the coming of globalisation and the
decline in the importance of the nation state; the
increasing importance of fundamentalism and
consumerism to the process of identity formation; the rise
of a global postmodern culture; the increasing importance
of new technology; and the speed-up of mass
communication through satellites and the internet, to
name some of the most important ones.

(Oliver, 2001, p. 153)

Michael Oliver is describing major changes within society as a whole.
'Fordism' is the name given to mass production using assembly-line
techniques in an urban-industrial society. 'Post-fordism' refers to new
methods of production, beyond the conveyor-belt, industrial model,
that will result in a pressure for the education system to teach the skills
needed for new ways of working.

The issue of globalization means that governments may have fewer
powers in contrast to the increasing influence of multi-national
companies. In 2002, out of the 100 biggest economic units on the
planet, 51 were corporations; the other 49 were countries. Trade
between subsidiaries within the same parent corporations accounted
for roughly a third of world trade (*New Internationalist*, 2002). The
education system has been intrinsically part of the nation state, a
discrete physical territory presided over by a government. In the
context of globalization, the power of the state and its influence on
education may change in ways we cannot yet foresee.

Economic factors are undoubtedly influencing government thinking
about the use of new technologies in education. In 1999 Prime
Minister Tony Blair argued:

The transformation ahead may be as significant as the rise
of organised schooling itself ... Entering the 21st century
with the new technology, our goal is to become 'learning
bound' not 'teacher bound' – not to replace teachers, but
to enhance and supplement them – in and out of school –
with the vast interactive resources of ICT. It has been
estimated that the full cost of one school teacher-hour is
£50 and, rightly for our teachers, it is rising; but the full
cost of one school ICT-hour is about 75p, and dropping at
20% a year, at the same time as the inherent capability of
the technology is rising. And as it rises, in the hands of
skilled teachers as learning managers, so too does the
capacity for ICT to personalise learning – to provide the
tailored support for different aptitudes and needs which is

critical to the future. This is one of the most exciting and important implications of ICT.

(Quoted in Hampshire County Council, 2003)

Universal design and individual assistance

Against this background, what might schools of the future look like? In 2002 a conference in the USA brought together scientists and technologists who were actively creating the technologies that would be most likely to shape our future. These new technologies, termed NBIC, are a mixture of nanotechnology (manipulating materials on a molecular scale to build microscopic devices), biotechnology, information technology, and cognitive technologies. The NBIC group saw a clear need for a change in educational practices and they saw technology as a key part of this 'age of transition'.

> [T]oday's schools combine an agricultural-era nine- or ten-month school year (including the summer off for harvesting) with an industrial era 50-minute class, with a 'foreman' at the front of the room facing a class of 'workers' in a factory-style school day, in a Monday-to-Friday work week. Learning in the future will be embedded in the computer and on the Internet and will be available on demand with a great deal of customization for each learner.

(Gingrick, 2002, pp. 48–9)

Another US presentation looked at how new technologies might affect human performance and produced several visions of what a future school would look like, including this:

> The year is 2015. You enter a ... school. From the outside, it appears to be much the same physical structure as schools were for 50 years. But inside is a totally different world. Teachers are busily meeting with one another and engaged in e-learning to stay current on the latest developments in education and their disciplines ... Science teachers are working in a cross-disciplinary program that has been particularly fruitful – NBIC – a wonderful stew of nanotechnology, biotechnology, information technology, and cognitive technologies ... A number of special needs students are working in rooms, receiving cues from a wireless network that are appropriate for their individual cognitive and physical needs as developed through NBIC ... Each student in the community can interact with other students worldwide to share information, language, and culture. While the student population of more than 50 million students has been joined by millions of parents as lifelong learning requirements are realized, no new buildings have been

required, as many students take advantage of 24/7 availability of coursework at their homes, in work areas, and at the school.

(Batterson and Pope, 2002, pp. 416–17)

▷ Activity 16.1   Leads for needs

Re-read the description of a school in 2015 quoted above and identify the elements that have changed significantly and those that have remained largely unchanged. Do you find this prediction convincing? Supposing it was realized, do you see anything wrong with it?

▷ In Batterson and Pope's vision new technologies allow both teachers and pupils to work more collaboratively. In addition, lifelong learning is established within the system. These elements fit with aspects of pedagogy that we identified as being inclusive in Units 5 and 13.

However, the authors have projected their current understanding of disability and special needs into the future, suggesting a view of disability and learning difficulties locked into a deficit model. This model, as we saw in Unit 2, originated in education early in the last century.

The fact that the building appears to be largely unchanged and 'a number of special needs students are working in rooms' suggests a segregation that contradicts the collaboration and interaction suggested elsewhere. It does seem to us to reflect a special needs rather than an inclusive vision of the future. The technology is used to further inequality.

Why mention this example? Well, as noted in Units 1 and 2, the beliefs of previous decades and centuries do not necessarily disappear with the dawning of a new period in history or technological advancement. Imagine someone at the turn of the previous century talking about the benefits of technological advances and new societies but carrying forward beliefs about apartheid and sex discrimination. The discourses of the past continue to act upon and influence how we act and therefore how we build the future. Thus, many people still believe that in order to improve the way we 'help pupils with special educational needs' we need to develop increasingly refined methods of identifying those needs and then produce technological solutions to meet them. This assistive technology (AT) approach is premised on a

particular view of disability and learning, a view which Alex, in the cartoon, has got the measure of.

There are, however, other discourses that point to different outcomes. These are the beginnings of alternative futures competing to come into existence. Universal design (UD), for example, begins with a premise of designing products and environments that can be used and experienced by people of all ages and abilities to the greatest extent possible without adaptation (Universal Design Institute, 2003).

Both AT and UD are currently being developed. A crucial difference is that UD begins from a premise of diversity and accommodation (which is much more a move towards how we see inclusion), whereas AT begins with a perspective of individual special needs and then attempts to enable assimilation. If we start from a universal standpoint, fewer individual designs will be needed and everyone might potentially benefit. This sort of development of technology could also become an analogy to be used in constructing inclusive curricula and schools.

Activity 16.2 Marmalade in the twenty-first century

As I was writing this I paused to have some toast and marmalade, but found that I couldn't open the jar. Various family members tried to help. They also failed. Some had hands that were too small and another had physical impairments that meant they couldn't apply pressure. Two people suggested inserting a spike below the cap to break the vacuum, but one couldn't do this because they were too young to use sharp knives and the other couldn't see well enough to do it. Together we eventually opened the jar.

How might we find solutions to this problem through the two technological approaches – assistive technology and universal design – discussed above. Brainstorm some solutions. You might wish to explain the task to a friend and ask them for their suggestions, or see what they think of yours.

 Here are some of our ideas.

The assistive technology approach

The user of the jar is weak and needs to develop their physical strength. That is their problem, but they can do exercises.

There are special devices to open jars. Get them one of those. That will sort them out. There's a shop somewhere that sells them. I'll ask the occupational therapist. She'll know.

The universal design approach

Produce a jar that could be opened by almost anyone: a self-unscrewing jar or a flip-top one. Perhaps a big button on the lid to release the vacuum.

Marmalade in a tube, or ready-marmaladed toast, like ready-made meals.

The manufacturers should just make sure that the jar is easy to open. They're not all impossible, are they? Make them like that and check all the jars properly.

· ·

This light-hearted example raised many of the ideas that we discussed in previous units – normalization, special approaches and curtailment of choice ('Don't eat marmalade.' 'I don't like it anyway.' 'You won't miss it.'). When we explained this activity to a friend, they said that the universal design idea had no relevance to inclusive education because it was really about inclusion in general – trying to change society rather than helping people learn and change themselves.

It's not the business of education to 'redesign marmalade jars' and presumably alter the factories (and profits) of companies that make them. It doesn't work that way round. A school's job is to get the person the skills to open the jar, with or without aid, and to function in the real world. We live in the real world and some disabled children would require special help, obviously, no matter what you did.

Our counter-argument was that people are disabled *by* the design of the jar, to which the friend retorted that the jar was normal and anyone who couldn't open it was not normal and therefore needed help. 'That's how things are.' This way of thinking has, we believe, helped to create and maintain disabling features within the built and social environments. The special needs model lends itself to a split between what is education and what is not, a split which doesn't arise in the universal design approach, which sees disability not as a characteristic of an individual but as emerging from an interaction between people and their environment.

> If education is going to be re-created in the new society to which we are moving and going back is impossible, then it is also inevitable that special education will be transformed by that process of re-creation ...
>
> The way in which debates in special education have moved ... onto what has come to be called the inclusion/ exclusion debate is indicative of the fact that this debate, once narrowly confined to education is now about the possibility of an inclusive society.
>
> *(Oliver, 2001, p. 157)*

In other words, this change of thinking leads us to adopt a wider view of education. In the 'split' vision, education is a means of social control; in the unified view, education is one part of a movement of social change. Inclusive education develops as a disabling society is transformed.

The ends justify the memes

We have introduced the idea that many possible futures compete to come into existence. One way of understanding how the future is shaped is by examining the way in which ideas are transmitted between people and how they change, or evolve, and gain currency over time. The concept of 'memes' has become established in this context. Anne Campbell explains:

> Evolution is a process of change over time, and it doesn't have to apply only to genes – it could be human ideas.
>
> *(Campbell, 2003)*

Ideas, and the things we do, can be seen as units of cultural information that are passed between people and multiply. At the same time, those that do not get passed on eventually become extinct and disappear.

In *The Selfish Gene* (1989) Richard Dawkins described memes as including ideas, catch phrases, fashions, melodies, ways of making pots, starting fires or of building arches. If a meme 'catches on', then it spreads itself across brains. The person becomes a vehicle for propagating the meme in the same way as they are a vehicle for propagating their biological genes.

> Memes should be regarded as living structures, not just metaphorically but technically. When you plant a fertile meme in my mind, you literally parasitize my brain, turning it into a vehicle for the meme's propagation in just the way that a virus may parasitize the genetic mechanism of a host cell. And this isn't just a way of talking – the meme for, say, 'belief in life after death' is actually realized physically, millions of times over, as a structure in the nervous systems of people all over the world.
>
> *(Dawkins, 1989, p. 192)*

So, for inclusion to take root in our thinking about education there needs to be an 'inclusive meme', or groups of memes, that support inclusive practices and propagate themselves within the minds of a large number of people.

One can make a link between discourses and memes. Bruce Dorries and Beth Haller's analysis of the media coverage of an educational court case in 'The news of inclusive education: a narrative analysis' (Chapter 23 in Reader 1) uncovers several narrative themes, some of which might be regarded as 'inclusive memes', for example, 'human rights should apply to everyone in a civilized society'. However, inclusive memes will need to propagate more successfully than non-inclusive memes such as 'Not in my kids' school' (Dorries and Haller, in Reader 1, p. 285), which carries and spreads the assumption that inclusive education will always have a disruptive effective on non-disabled children and should therefore not be allowed. Peter Ritchie (2000) identifies a current, pervasive anti-inclusive meme.

> The meme ... is believing that the world is divided into two groups of people – them and us. Different rules apply to them, they are made differently. They feel things differently. Any characteristic will do for separating them from us – religion, gender, ethnic origin, age, impairment or even postcode. Once we have made this separation, the problem becomes focused on them.
>
> *(Ritchie, 2000)*

It has been suggested that the influence of memes is more significant in producing educational change than deliberate attempts to reform education. For example:

the concept of learning disability entered School in a manner more akin to the way that memes invade cultures than to the conduct of an education reform movement; institutionalization from above followed the cultural movement.

(Papert, 1997a, pp. 417–18)

As memes are passed along they can become distorted to carry ideas and meanings that they did not originally hold. For example, the words might stay the same while their meaning is hijacked or parasitized to produce different outcomes from the original.

Local authorities are actually cutting back on their provision for the most challenging children. Government responses to the howls of complaints from the profession have focused on in-school provision: 'inclusion units' where children can be isolated for part of the day.

(Revell, 2003)

This phenomenon may explain why Roger Slee raised the possibility that an apparent shift to inclusive education 'connotes a linguistic adjustment to present a politically correct façade to a changing world' (Slee, quoted in Oliver, 2001, p. 157). The underlying practices carry on, in a reconstructed version of 'inclusion'.

Just as the physical environment affects the selection of genes, so the social environment affects the selection and survival of memes. The education system as it stands will act upon the memes that it encounters and affect how likely it is that they are passed on. Some memes are quickly and easily assimilated into the school system: for example, back to basics, focus on the 3 Rs, and testing standards. Others require accommodation, with some significant changes being needed in a part of the system. Because there are many interrelated parts of a school system, this can create a tension. There is a force that pulls away from change (Papert, 1997a). The system selects which memes survive within it, in the same way that the environment selects which biological genes are passed on. It is likely to reject the meme, change it to fit, or find a meme that fits better.

So, will there be an inclusive meme that propagates and lives into the future? This unit, and E243 itself, might be seen as a meme propagator. Perhaps one meme from the unit so far is the concept of universality – 'the concept that some things hold for all of us, whatever our age, whatever our ethnic origins, whatever our impairments' (Ritchie, 2000). Perhaps another can be found within the unit title: 'Some memes make our brains do work by having more than one meaning, like 'Imagine Better' (Ritchie, 2000).

◯ Activity 16.3   Schools without walls

Now read Chapter 10 in Reader 1, 'Has classroom teaching served its day?' by Donald McIntyre.

McIntyre describes the limitations of the current system and indicates some areas where changes are needed. As you read McIntyre's discussion consider the implications of such changes for inclusive education.

One feature that emerged for us in McIntyre's discussion was the way that the system itself acts to limit what is possible through classroom teaching, even where teachers have the skills and motivation to act otherwise. For example, the system maintains beliefs about general ability and models of assessment that may act against pupils' opportunities for learning. For pupils with learning difficulties, such constraints have had a tremendous impact on their school lives.

The way ahead, as McIntyre sees it, includes much more active involvement for pupils in their own learning, in both the curriculum and the organization of the school. Further, he sees learning as moving out of the classroom, supported by 'computers and modern technology'. It is interesting that although they do not specifically address inclusive education, McIntyre's ideas support the arguments developed about inclusive practices in Units 7, 8 and 13. We would certainly see a more inclusive system evolving from the development of a better education for all.

3 New technology and responsive environments

The discussion of models of learning in Unit 8 suggested that some approaches are much more supportive of inclusion than others. One important aspect is building on the pupil's interests and knowledge and responding to them. Technology has often been used to drive objectivist, outside-in approaches to learning. In this way, technology has been assimilated into the system to fit with existing teaching practices. However, as information and communications technology (ICT) becomes more sophisticated it has the potential to operate in new, constructivist ways. Where might this lead?

In describing what online education has to offer, Greg Kearsley (2000) presents the following concepts that can be used to think about inclusive education and learning in general:

- *Collaboration* – the new technologies support collaboration among students and teachers. Collaboration will become easier between pairs or within whole classes, or between different classes.

- *Connectivity* – people and information are available online. Information can be accessed directly and quickly. If you have an interest you can find out about it.

- *Student-centredness* – teachers may define goals and facilitate the learning process, but students are increasingly able to discover content on their own. The responsibility for learning becomes more shared than previously. This may lead to student-defined learning goals.

- *Community* – real and virtual communities can be supported and built with relative ease. 'It is possible to create a virtual school or college that consists of a learning community with no actual buildings' (Kearsley, 2000, p. 7). (As you will see when you read Chapter 11, in Reader 1, in the next activity, this type of change creates issues about the nature of inclusion.)

- *Exploration* – the opportunities are expanded for problem-based learning and learning through discovery.

- *Shared knowledge* – students are able to access an enormous range of information and they can also publish and contribute towards this shared knowledge network.

- *Multi-sensory experience* – options are developing to expand the way we present and manipulate information, from text for reading to virtual reality environments.

- *Authenticity* – correlated with connectivity, community and shared knowledge, online education can give students authentic experiences. Students can access actual databases, view through webcams and talk to experts and to children from other countries. Further, they will be able to carry out work that has an intrinsic value. 'The lack of realism in traditional instruction has often been identified as a major weakness of education at all levels' (Kearsley, 2000, p. 10).

In Neal Stephenson's (2000) fictional story *The Diamond Age* a designer creates a 'teaching machine' about the same size and shape as a book. It is stolen and falls into the hands of a young girl who lives in poverty and neglect. The 'book' has certain teaching strategies. It is interactive, multi-sensory and builds upon the girl's life experiences. It adapts itself to her developing interests and abilities and to what she needs to learn to survive in the world. It builds knowledge with the girl in a way that is genuinely interesting and relevant for her. Through the machine she also learns how to learn. In many ways the machine represents the qualities of good 'human' teaching. Although the development of this fictional machine may seem a long way off, technology is developing quickly and approaches such as interactive multimedia, graphical simulations, and game-like virtual reality are being aimed at.

> Thus we will need new kinds of curricula, such as interactive virtual reality simulations run over the Internet that will allow a student anywhere to experience the metabolic processes that take place within a living cell, as if seeing them from a nanoscale perspective ... The social interaction resulting from multiuser video games can be harnessed as a strong learning motivator, if they are designed for the user's demographic and cultural background and can infuse the learning with mystery, action, and drama.

> *(Bainbridge et al., 2002, p. 100)*

In the Blue Peter/Open University RoboFesta robot design competition children were challenged to design a really useful robot that could make 'a positive contribution to human life'. The children were encouraged to be 'creative and focus their energies on something constructive, in contrast to the *robot wars* genre of programs which [was, at the time], very popular on television in Britain' (Johnson and Hirst, 2001). Figures 16.1, 16.2 and 16.3 show three of the entries.

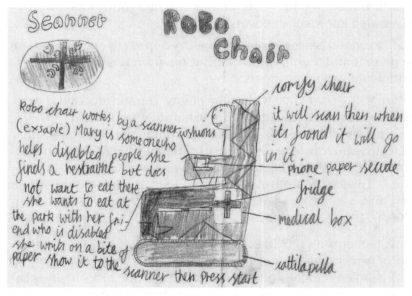

Figure 16.1   RoboFesta design competition entry: Mary's Robo chair.

Both young children and cutting-edge designers see developments in ICT as having the potential to improve our lives and experiences of education. How real-life technological developments relate specifically to inclusion is an important question to consider. The next activity addresses this.

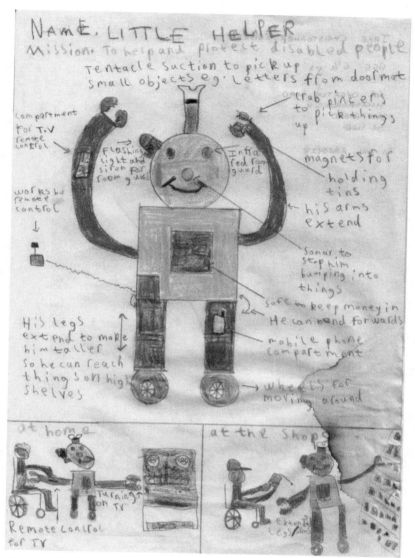

Figure 16.2   *RoboFesta design competition entry: Little Helper.*

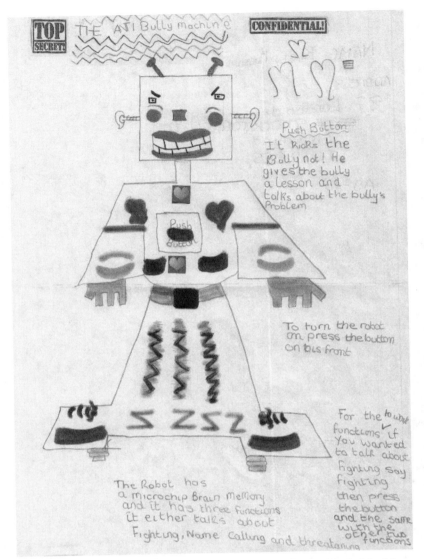

Figure 16.3   RoboFesta design competition entry: The Anti-Bully Machine.

Activity 16.4   New technology and inclusion

Read Chapter 11 in Reader 1, 'New technology and inclusion: the world (wide web) is not enough' by Kieron Sheehy. As you read, identify the relationship that the author sees between technology and society. You might also wish to consider whether the view taken is a balanced one regarding the benefits of technology in supporting inclusion.

Although it presents some possible negative aspects, this chapter does end up painting quite an optimistic picture of the potential of new technology. Given, for example, the negative uses to which the internet can be put, you might disagree with this positive viewpoint. The chapter argues that the way in which technology is used is culturally embedded. Awareness of this can help us to develop more inclusive practices and reduce the likelihood of transferring discriminatory practices into our usage of new technologies. Such an awareness is vital, as discriminatory memes are often deeply enmeshed. As the following case study illustrates, they can be so much part and parcel of the things we do that they pass unnoticed.

A case study of a Trojan Horse

As we are writing this unit, in 2003, a piece of software is being marketed. It is a 'multimedia literacy development programme'. The software itself builds on many established elements of practice and uses the advantages of ICT to give the learner auditory feedback combined with the visual presentation of words. It would appear to be a great resource for any classroom and it certainly seems to be making good use of ICT to support learning.

However, the content of the reading exercises carries memes from a different era. Females are passive and usually nameless, while the men are active, creative, clever, brave, successful and important. People from the 'East, Africa, South America' are associated with the phrases 'masses of miserable half-starved people', 'impossible for their governments to cope' and 'need outside help'. Native Americans are referred to as 'The Indians' and a 'backward, simple race' (McGee et al., 2000). The material fails to satisfy the criteria and recommendations of reports concerned with sex-roles and sex-stereotyping (for example, DES, 1994) with regard to language, content, roles and character or ethnicity and racism.

How is it that such material can pass into use so easily? There are several possible reasons. First, the target group for the software is pupils with dyslexia. If there is a focus on this single aspect of the person, then other aspects may be less likely to be considered. Second, the technology itself acts to mask these aspects of the software; we are drawn to focus on the structure and multi-media aspects of the technology. It isn't seen as 'reading material' as such. Third, the organization that produces the material is a charity, outside of the state education system and therefore not subject to the checks of 'the system'. Finally, good software is hard to come by. If it does 'the job', then perhaps we might overlook its flaws. If the pupil is seen in terms of a single attribute or impairment, then such overlooking may be more likely to occur because 'the job' is to sort out the child's reading.

Artificial intelligence in education

The software described in the previous section largely used computer-based instruction to develop traditional methods of learning and teaching. As discussed in Reader 1, Chapter 11, such programs often use drill and practice with high-quality feedback on performance in order to reach well-defined goals for learning. However, the use of new technologies in the service of traditional methods and learning goals of teaching is making less and less sense. As David McArthur and his colleagues argue:

> most successful educational technology in the future must be part of a larger technology revolution ... As technologies in the workplace – and our culture in general – begin to reshape valued educational goals, they will also redefine the available resources for education ... they will permit us to consider a wide range of new methods of teaching and learning, and perhaps also to realize old methods – like individualized tutoring – that we have always believed to be valuable, but that hitherto have been too costly to implement on a wide scale.

> (McArthur et al., 1993)

David McArthur et al. suggest that there is a build-up of pressure from outside the school system of new ideas and practices that will act to produce change within the classroom. In the same way that the industrial era and production-lines shaped education, the new post-industrial era of the twenty-first century will also shape practices within schools (Lipsky and Gartner, 1997).

This change would place new demands on teachers and learners as ideas of what teaching and learning is all about are challenged. New technology, and artificial inteligence (AI) in particular, can rejuvenate existing methods such as apprenticeships and one-on-one tutoring, but also provide a foundation for completely new methods of acquiring knowledge (McArthur *et al.*, 2002). As suggested in Reader 1, Chapter 11, these new methods are seen as having much greater potential to support the development of inclusive education.

The use of computer-based programs to interact with humans is not new. 'Eliza', a computer program designed to act as an online counsellor, responding to input from people, was part of a trend to develop intelligent and responsive programs that began in the mid-1960s (Murray, 1997). Indeed, some of Eliza's 'daughters' could pass as being non-machine in certain online interactions. Janet Murray (1997) describes 'Julia', a 'chatterbot', or program that carries on conversations in an online environment. So persuasive were Julia's abilities that one poor human suitor, Barry, spent thirteen days unsuccessfully trying to 'woo' her. Julia is also an expert conversationalist on a limited number of topics and can generate 'knowledgeable' responses from a large information database. Within a specific virtual context 'she' works well. The use of robots in therapy is, however, a relatively recent phenomenon.

The AURORA project explores 'if and how a mobile robot can be used to encourage pro-active communication in a child by studying unconstrained interactions between a child and a mobile robot in a playful context' (Dautenhahn and Werry, 2001). The robot is autonomous and capable of producing words or simple phrases in particular situations. The robot can also avoid obstacles and detect and follow humans.

The primary aim of this research and the thinking behind it are described as follows:

> We believe that since autonomy is an important factor in *human–human* social interaction it is also important for recognizing and accepting a *machine* as an interaction partner ...

> [The aim] is not to develop a social relationship between the robot and the child. Ultimately, the robot should play the role of a mediator, a device that can help a child to bond with other (autistic or non-autistic) people ...

> The AURORA project aims at teaching children with autism social skills. Generally, learning about social skills in the AURORA project should be a positive, 'joyful' experience.

> *(Dautenhahn and Werry, 2001)*

▷ # Activity 16.5   Robots and therapy

How do you feel about the AURORA project type of research and its aims? Imagine that you were arguing for the development of this work. Make a note of some of the points that you'd use to support it. Then consider arguments against this type of approach. You might like to share these thoughts with a friend and see if you can build on them.

▷ Our thoughts on this included the following:

We'd be happy for children to use a responsive computer program to learn a skill such as reading or how to sing in tune. This robot thing is no different really. The skill is one of social communication. It's just that the computer's hardware moves about and has unlimited patience. If the child learns the skills they need, then that's what matters.

The approach uses the language of therapy to justify testing out machines on a vulnerable group. Why not test it on managers or members of Parliament? Because their time is seen as more valuable and they have the power to say no?

Why not use humans to teach human interaction skills? That would seem much more sensible.

This is about technology rather than children, and perhaps economics too, justified by the therapy label.

This is bad special education dressed up as innovation, or it's trying to replicate something that humans can do anyway for the sake of the robots rather than the children.

One of our beliefs is that we need to build on our human ability to interact rather than on alternatives, so we would be concerned that 'human interaction' might be constrained or even replaced by the influence of technology. Why are we seeking computers or robots to do something that human beings do better? Human beings have infinite potential to be responsive to others and so to develop interactions that are meaningful for children with autism.

In their work on intensive interaction, Melanie Nind and colleagues discuss the ways in which human beings can be regarded as 'hard-wired' for social interaction (Nind and Hewett, 1994; Nind and Powell, 2000). They argue that although children with autism, for example, may leave us feeling unskilled and unconfident, if we are to enhance our social relationships it is our human ability to interact that we need to develop rather than alternatives. From this perspective, our future investment might be in human resources rather than in technology. This point is not made about teaching in general, but

Figure 16.4   A Snoezelen room.

about the teaching and communication of social abilities in particular.

In considering the future, then, it is worth pausing to think about whether technology always offers a better alternative. Another question is whether we have thought about the teaching and learning first, and the technology second. In recent decades there has been considerable growth in the popularity of multi-sensory, or snoezelen, rooms for individuals with profound learning difficulties or autism.

Snoezelen rooms (See Figure 16.4) are environments with pleasing light and sound effects, moving images, and so on, that can be controlled by voluntary or involuntary movement. Much faith, as well as money, has been invested in these without equal attention having been given to how they contribute to teaching and learning. As with many 'advances', it may be that we have gone down this route largely because we can. We are also seduced by the legacy of special education thinking – that something different and special is needed (Thomas and Loxley, 2001) – rather than thinking about all the multi-sensory and cause and effect opportunities that are offered by ordinary peers and ordinary environments.

4   Diversity, disability and choice

One promise that the future appears to offer us is that of greater choice about 'who we are'. Chapter 11 in Reader 1, 'New technology and inclusion', suggested, for example, that in cyberspace we will have more control over how we express and construct our identities. This potential is set against a background of demographic changes. A survey of school children in Greater London showed that over a quarter spoke a language other than English at home (Centre for Racial Equality, 2003). Yasmin Hussain and colleagues (2002) discuss how South Asian young deaf people in Scotland and the north of England have a number of potential identity claims, including: ethnicity, religion, Deaf, linguistic, disabled, young person. Hussain *et al.*'s research suggests that young people's choices about describing 'who they are' do not rely on a singular identity such as 'Muslim' or 'Scottish'. 'Instead, young people's identifications were multiple, and complex' (Hussain *et al.*, 2002). This trend is likely to continue.

So, we may choose to construct alternative 'virtual' identities and can draw on different aspects of our culture and background in deciding who we are. Developments in the area of biological science, and possibly nanotechnology, could offer greater choice in the development of our physical bodies. This might include developing intelligent artificial devices to replace or extend parts of the body, either external or internal. We are already familiar with pacemakers that send electrical impulses to one's heart, but we are likely to go beyond this prosthetic approach.

This is shocking and frightening stuff to contemplate, especially in light of our inability to fully foresee the consequences of our actions ... While selective breeding of crops, animals, and people (as in ancient Sparta) is many hundreds of generations old, only recently have gene therapies become possible as the inner working of the billion-year-old molecular tools of bacteria for slicing and splicing DNA have been harnessed by the medical and research communities ... soon we can expect other researchers building on these results to suggest ways of increasing the IQs of humans.

(Spohrer, 2002, pp. 111–12)

Being smart

We have yet to reach the permanent genetic engineering of intelligence. The quest to be smarter is currently seen in, for example, the marketing of smart drugs and nootropics. The term 'nootropics' was originally coined to describe the drug piracetam. Nootropics also include substances to prevent memory loss or boost intelligence, and the term is now used to describe an array of substances that might improve cognitive performance, including, for example, ginkgo biloba and antioxidants such as vitamin E. A growing number of 'brain boosters' are being developed. The concept of 'smarter' in this context is usually related to performance in IQ tests of one form or another (see Unit 2). But as we have discussed, the culture in which knowledge is created is important.

The unique development of the human mind is an adaptation to *social* problem-solving; and the selective advantages it brings. Yet pharmaceuticals that enhance our capacity for empathy, or enrich our social skills, or deepen our introspective self-knowledge, are not conventional candidates for smart drugs. For such faculties don't reflect our traditional [male] scientific value-judgements on what qualifies as 'intelligence'. Emotional literacy is certainly harder to quantify scientifically than mathematical puzzle-solving ability or performance in verbal memory-tests. But before chemically manipulating one's mind, it's worth critically examining which capacities one wants to enhance; and to what end?

(The Golden House-Sparrow Award, 2001)

The best place to begin 'intellectual boosting' would surely be with the eradication of poverty, a healthy lifestyle that included regular aerobic activity, a sensible diet, positive social interactions and a more social view of ability. In contrast to such a universal design approach is the lure of assistive technology in the form of nootropics, and smart drugs. This approach is embedded in a competitive hierarchical ethos, reflected here in the lyrics of Momus's 1996 song *Smart Drugs*.

Smart drugs keep me up with the hackers
Smart drugs keep me from cracking up
Keep me up with the pack
Anything I can do you can do too
Keep your eyes open for anything new
Fantastic dimensions in space time for the brain
Open up all the time
See what the boys in the valley are taking and tell them
I'm taking ...
Nyacin, piracetam, hydergine and sixteen more nutropics
at recommended dosage

(*Momus, quoted in Phespirit, 2003*)

Here, smart drugs are a way of keeping up, or, more important, keeping ahead. It is an approach that focuses entirely on the rational-intellectual, ignoring physical and emotional well-being. Yet the emotional and social aspects of learning are essential to our development (Collins *et al.*, 2002); to focus entirely on the development of one aspect of our selves is as poor a strategy as treating people in terms of a single label. We would argue for an approach that is person-centred and participative, one that considers the learner as a whole person.

 # Activity 16.6   Pills for ills

As one would expect, there has been a strong interest in research with nootropics and children with learning difficulties, for example, in the use of piracetam for children with Down syndrome. The extract below is from the transcript of a 1997 television programme.

As you read the extract, identify the purpose that nootropics are seen as serving. In your learning journal jot down both the way in which discourses position the use of the drugs and also the types of discourses used. For example, do opposing arguments necessarily use a different discourse to those that advocate drug use? Are you persuaded by either argument? When might you consider giving nootropics to a child? If you were a child what would you want to do?

. . . . *Extract from CBS 48 Hours: 'Hype or hope?'* . . . . .

Tonight, one mother's relentless struggle to improve her child's life ...
(*Voiceover*) I want my child [to] have a totally complete life. She's got a right to grow up and walk down that aisle and hold her own children in her arms if she wants ...

(Voiceover) What Dixie Lawrence Tafoya wants for adopted daughter Madison … doesn't seem all that unusual … until you realize that Madison was born with Down syndrome.

And I don't want chronic illness or a foggy brain anything to stand in her way …

I was in love with her beyond anything I've ever felt, and it was imperative to me to know everything that I could about her disease. And it is a disease …

(Voiceover) She's a housewife … who single-handedly convinced a team [of] doctors and scientists to create a treatment for Down syndrome.

we studied the blood and urine of over 4,000 patients with Down syndrome …

(Voiceover) Madison has been taking Nutrivene-D and piracetam for over four years with what Dixie claims are startling results …

(Voiceover) She's seven years old. She's supposed to be mentally retarded. Her cognitive abilities and her intellect are as a child without Down syndrome.

(Voiceover) Very much like a normal seven year-old's …

(Voiceover) Dixie says the treatment has also changed her daughter's appearance.

(Pointing to photo) OK. Madison's mouth – instead of being downturned – her muscle tone increased to the point where she could have a more normal smile. This little girl's in la-la land and this little girl (pointing to different photo) – she looks like she's more in tune with her world …

(Voiceover) The pictures are evidence enough for thousands of parents Dixie has been able to reach on the Internet …

(Voiceover) Why is it not OK for my daughter to have Down syndrome? Why? Why is it not OK for Emily to have Down syndrome? …

(Voiceover) Not all parents … of children with Down syndrome are impressed with Dixie Tafoya's theories … Down syndrome is not a terminal illness. It's just Emily.

(Voiceover) … nor are they willing to chance an untested treatment on their children.

I don't think it's safe. I myself wouldn't use a drug that has never been tested. It's very scary to me that these people are doing this to their child.

(Voiceover) Cindy Urso's child, Ashley, is six.

Come on, Ash. I love my daughter the way she is. I wouldn't change her for anything in the world.

(Extract from a transcript of a show broadcast by CBS, Down Syndrome: Health Issues, 2003)

· ·

▷ There seem to be at least two discourses being expressed here. The first is one of normalization through treatment: the child is different and will not be socially valued as such; drugs can cure this and open up the potential for a normal life; this is simple and risk-free. Therefore, not to give the child the drug can be seen as neglect.

One counter-argument also uses this medical/deficit view, but notes that the drugs haven't been sufficiently tested. Another discourse is more accepting of diversity: children 'are who they are' and it is society that needs to change. This view reflects the social model of disability.

· ·

Normalization has been a strong influence in social and educational policy for people with learning difficulties. Although it encompasses a range of approaches, normalization advocates the social integration of people with learning difficulties by creating 'an existence ... as close to normal living conditions as possible ... making normal mentally retarded people's housing, education, working and leisure conditions' (Bank-Mikkelson, quoted in Culham and Nind, 2003), with typical patterns of daily activities for a person of their age. This idea had many positive effects, particularly in the provision of community-based services (Culham and Nind, 2003). However, the ideas of gaining access to the full opportunities and facilities of society became entwined with a striving to 'fit in'. The patterns and activities of being 'normal' were implied to be morally better. This led to an acceptance of changing 'the behaviour, appearance, and even preferences of people with an intellectual disability in the name of achieving their integration and valued role' (Cullham and Nind, 2003, p. 71).

In the future we will have the power to change people to a far greater degree. Smart drugs are just the beginning. Physical surgery for cosmetic reasons has become commonplace; gene therapy is on the way. Normalization in this context is becoming an easier option to impose and can act to support the denial of difference and diversity. In the future, those supporting inclusion will need to consider how they respond to normalization 'options'.

You will have thought of other responses to the transcript. Debates such as these are likely to become more common in future as the possibilities for chemical, prosthetic and genetic change increase. The case for and against the use of Ritalin as a treatment for Attention Deficit Hyperactivity Disorder has been debated widely in the media. While this debate continues, the number of children prescribed the drug increases. Prescriptions of Ritalin in England went up from 2,000 in 1991, to 2,600 in 1992, to 92,000 in 1997 (Stuftaford, quoted in Monk, 2000), 140,000 in 1999 and 230,000 in 2002 (*The Guardian*, 2003).

> This practice illustrates the extent to which social pathology is treated as individual illness, and demonstrates how medical knowledge and expertise operate as a technique of modern government that serve to legitimise the problematization of child behaviour that deviates from the norm.
>
> *(Monk, 2000, p. 361)*

As the possibilities for changing people increase, the boundaries of what should be discussed under 'education' will alter. The more aspects of our being that are seen as 'treatable', the more pressure there might be from discourses of normalization. Could the supposedly inclusive school of the future actually be composed of a decreasingly diverse range of pupils? Or will choices be linked to an ability to pay, and therefore reflect social and economic differences?

Making decisions

A key question within this discussion is how decisions will be reached regarding the use of new treatments or technologies. The following quotation highlights this aspect of the future.

> Science and technology (S&T) have had throughout history – and will have in the future – positive and negative consequences for humankind ... S&T activity is the result of human activity imbued with intention and purpose and embodying the perspectives, purposes, prejudice and particular objectives of any given society in which the research takes place ... The development of Bio/ Gene/Nanotechnology is – among other things – justified with the argument that it holds the promises to fix or help to fix perceived disabilities, impairments, diseases, and defects and to diminish suffering. But who decides what is a disability, disease, an impairment and a 'defect' in need of fixing? Who decides what the mode of fixing (medical or societal) should be, and who decides what is suffering? How will these developments affect societal structures?
>
> *(Wolbring, 2002, p. 232)*

As we enter the age of 'new genetics', in which the human genome is being mapped, it is becoming possible to identify an increasing number of the features and attributes of unborn children. Patricia Rock is one of many people who note the resurgence of eugenics.

> Disabled people are under threat for their very existence in our modern technological societies. Medical science

feels able to flex its muscles and power to abolish all life
where the unborn foetus may be imperfect or impaired.

(Rock, 1996, p. 121)

There are those who argue that progress in this area should be given
free reign and suffer no interference from either 'presidents or popes'
(James Watson, quoted in Derbyshire, 2003), that is, that no one has
the right to block the use of genetic knowledge. Watson, a joint
discoverer of the structure of DNA, stated:

> whether you want a child with Down's syndrome should
> be your choice ... If parents want a short child, a tall child,
> an aggressive child – they might think they are too
> passive – let them ...

> Everyone wants to enhance their life. I would have liked
> to have been born brighter. I always felt I was stupid when
> I was a child. We are going against human nature if you
> say we can't improve things.

(Watson, quoted in Derbyshire, 2003)

Watson's arguments imply that parental choices will result in a
diverse range of children who might all be equally valued. It is
interesting, however, that this Nobel Prize winner would want himself
to have been brighter and, of course, any such choice would have
been made *for* him and not *by* him. Quite apart from dismissing
societal factors, the sub-text of Watson's argument is that everyone
will want 'brighter' children. Current practices of differential screening
reflect what is valued and leads to comments such as those of Patricia
Rock. There are currently few examples of parents actively choosing
children with impairments, and, as Figure 16.5 illustrates, controversy
results when this does occur.

Activity 16.7   Engineering the perfect child

Briefly examine a current media description that looks at science
and technology's power to change children. This might be taken
from a newspaper, a television or radio programme or a website
(such as the example in Figure 16.5). The prevention or
enhancement of a particular attribute would be good examples to
look at. Consider the implications for the concept of inclusion and
inclusive education. You might wish to think about the following
questions.

What does your source of information imply about human
diversity and perfection? How are these technologies portrayed?
For whom are the results seen as being beneficial – parents,
society, the child? Whose voices are being expressed in the
description?

Having considered the attitudes being expressed about diversity, consider how these and the attitudes of the people who are being discussed might differ.

Couple 'choose' to have deaf baby

Sharon Duchesneau and Candy McCullough, who have both been deaf since birth, were turned down by a series of sperm banks they approached looking for a donor suffering from congenital deafness.

The couple, who have been together for eight years, then approached a family friend who was totally deaf, and had five generations of deafness in his family.

> 'I can't understand why anybody would want to bring a disabled child into the world.'
> *Nancy Rarus, member of staff at the US National Association for the Deaf*

> 'The real issue is not whether people are trying to design deaf babies, but how society currently denies deaf children to enjoy the same rights, responsibilities, opportunities and quality of life as everyone.'
> *Stephen Rooney, spokesman for the British Deaf Association*

> 'A hearing baby would be a blessing. A deaf baby would be a special blessing.'

The women, from Bethesda, Maryland, are both mental health therapists and deaf therapists.

They told *The Washington Post* they believed they would make better parents to a deaf child, because they would be better able to guide them.

They say their choice is no different from choosing what gender the child would be.

Ms McCullough added: 'Some people look at it like "Oh my gosh, you shouldn't have a child who has a disability". But you know, black people have harder lives. Why shouldn't people be able to go ahead and pick a black donor if that's what they want? They can feel related to that culture, still bonded with that culture.'

> 'We are saying no to deselecting a baby because it is deaf, and no to deliberately choosing to have a deaf baby. The principle could be extended to deliberately having a baby which was blind, or a dwarf.'
>
> **Peter Garrett, research director for LIFE**

Figure 16.5 Reactions in the media to parents actively choosing children with impairments (Source: BBC, 2002).

Many ethical questions arise in relation to these issues and it is important that those who have traditionally been marginalized in these debates become informed and active about them. The International Center for Bioethics, Culture and Disability takes this as its starting point. The Centre attempts to work on a global level to achieve its goals, which are:

- to examine the cultural aspects of bioethical issues and of science and technology,

- to examine the impacts of Bioethical issues and of science and technology on those who have been marginalized,

- to ensure that those who have been marginalized have a voice in all the debates that affect their lives,

- to help those who have been marginalized participate in the debates that affect their lives from a position of strength and knowledge,

- and to raise the capacity of those who have not been marginalized to welcome and understand the views of those who have been.

(International Center for Bioethics, Culture and Disability, 2003)

Information at this level is not necessarily power, but it is a much-needed advance towards it. Technology has acted both to create the issues and to provide a means of raising awareness and developing a shared understanding of their implications. Gregor Wolbring, founder of the International Center for Bioethics, Culture and Disability, highlights the importance of listening to the views of those who are often marginalized and the potential role of technology as a positive force.

Being a disabled person and being a scientist (biochemist/ bioethicist) led me to believe that a wide open public debate on how science and technology affects society and marginalized characteristics is the only way to develop safeguards against abuse. I believe that the dialog between the policy makers and the stakeholders has to increase ... I also try to increase the visibility of people with marginalized characteristics in these debates on governmental, academic, civil society, national or international level.

(Wolbring, 2003)

5 Conclusion

A lot will have happened since you began Unit 1 of E243, including things that you hadn't expected. Compared to yourself then, you are now in the future. Your learning on this course has interacted with your broader life. Many factors, events, incidents and your own history will have combined to produce the person that is now reading this and the way in which you have responded to, challenged and developed the ideas presented.

In sharing some ideas about the future of inclusive education, we have, of course, been selective. We may have left out or not emphasized areas that you would consider to be of great importance, for example, the impact of spirituality on society, changing demographics, fundamentalism, politics, education at home, architecture or lifestyles. You will have your own ideas and you may wish to discuss and develop them further. We hope that this unit has given you an impetus to do this.

Three themes

Three linked themes ran through this unit. The first is that technological developments will influence the society in which we live and the way we think about doing things. This new way of thinking will create new models for considering classroom practices and also offer us the tools for supporting new practices. The second theme is that, potentially, these new ways of doing things can be far more inclusive. This could move our practices beyond the groups we currently associate with the term 'inclusion' and allow us to teach all learners more effectively. Learners can become seen not in terms of a single, labelled attribute, but as people first. The third theme is that, in the long term, education will develop to be 'better' and that this 'better' education can be built on inclusive principles and values.

Whether we use the new technologies or not, the practices that emerge from them can transform the way we go about teaching and learning. It's not simply that we need to do things differently in order to use new technologies, but, more important, the new technologies provide us with different ways of thinking about teaching and learning. These ideas have a lot in common with the collaborative, student-centred principles and practices we constructed in Unit 13 as being inclusive and can offer a significant impetus to the development of inclusive education. It might well be that ideas emerging from our use of technology begin to change schools, through supporting inclusive practices, before the technology itself actually arrives in the classroom! New technology might facilitate inclusive education, but it is not a prerequisite.

Of course, any changes in the field of education occur within an economic, political and cultural context. You may feel that the pressures that resist change or challenge diversity will subvert movements towards inclusive education and act to further inequalities. This position is clearly stated by Rachael Hurst:

> For disabled people the impact of globalization has been to increase our isolation, our disempowerment, emphasize our difference and demonstrate our segregation from the rest of humanity. These negative impacts have also come from: global genetic advances and assessments of our quality of life; the multinational pharmaceutical companies' hold over research, patenting and genetic advances; the invisibility of disabled people from mainstream activity and information; and the silence of our voice in the corridors of power and change. We have a long way to go before the justice needed within globalization can celebrate our difference and ensure our humanity.
>
> *(Hurst, 2003, p. 164)*

There are certainly large barriers to be overcome and a need for considerable imagination and enthusiasm to see the immense potential that exists for positive change. However, such potential does exist. Imagine someone transported from twenty years ago into the present seeing new technology for the first time. In a sense, one such person was Nelson Mandela.

> [W]hat struck me so forcefully was how small the world had become during my decades in prison. [ICT] had shrunk the world, and had in the process become a great force for eradicating ignorance and promoting democracy.
>
> *(Mandela, 1995)*

Seymour Papert (1997b), considered the potential of computers in education and used a parable about the early days of powered flight. We would suggest that this analogy is also applicable to the development of inclusive education. Papert imagines a brilliant engineer inventing the jet engine around 1800. In practical terms it would be a laughable alternative to the horse-drawn wagon. However, people with imagination could see it as the start of an industry leading to space shuttles and jumbo jets. Thinking about the future of education, Papert suggests, demands a similar imaginative effort. It is easier to remain with a focus of 'what you see is what you get' and measure the effectiveness of technology in education by its current achievements and uses. This thinking makes tomorrow the prisoner of yesterday. Papert argues that this is like attaching a jet engine to an old fashioned wagon to see if it will help the horses. Most probably it would frighten the animals and shake the wagon to pieces, 'proving' that jet technology is actually harmful to the enhancement of transportation.

We would not want the development of inclusive education to be a 'prisoner to yesterday' and shackled by the pragmatics of the present, to be held accountable in terms of normalization, integration and 'special needs'. As Figures 16.6 and 16.7 show, children themselves have visions of how things could be different.

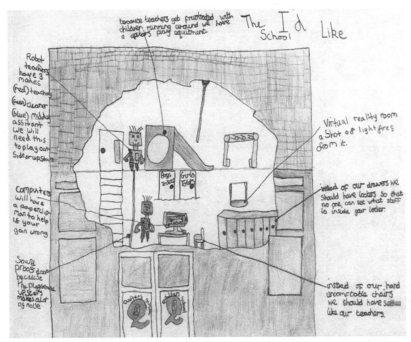

Figure 16.6   A Child's vision of the school they'd like (source: Burke and Grosvenor, 2003, p. 78).

The principles of powered flight were needed to inform the ways in which generations of people turned their ideas about flying into a reality. Even those who agreed that flight was possible disagreed about how best to go about achieving it and how far one might eventually be able to travel. In this course we have explored contested views about what inclusive education is and how to achieve it. We would argue that the principles have been established and, if we choose to do so, we can build from them.

> The school I'd like would stand for freedom, tolerance and flexibility. The school would be run by the whole learning community. Members of the community would support and respect each other, and nobody would be victimised or humiliated. There would be an atmosphere of cohesion and unity, avoiding segregation where possible. Students would be able to learn at their own

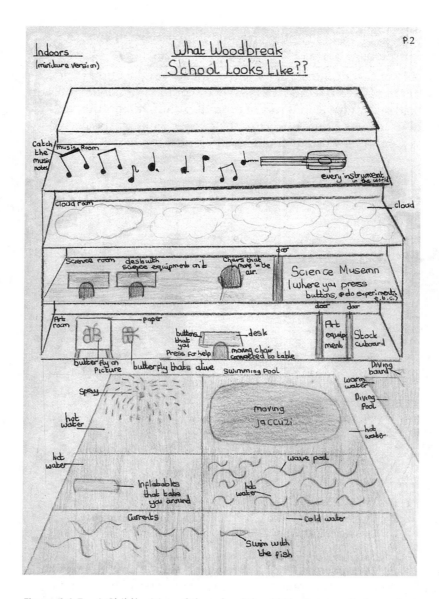

Figure 16.7   A Child's vision of the school they'd like (source: Burke and Grosvenor, 2003, p. 56).

pace, the school acknowledging their differing circumstances. All people would be valued, and enabled to develop their own abilities to the full, whether these be practical, academic, social, physical or artistic. It would be a place where students of all ages came voluntarily, because they actually wanted to be there

(Lorna, 14, in Burke and Grosvenor, 2003, p. 156)

A disabling society is reflected in the schools it creates. Our argument about universal design includes an assumption that the development of inclusive education does not occur separately from the development of an inclusive society, but is part of that process. The shape of the future will be influenced by how well inclusive ideals are advanced by those who care about them.

Communication and collaboration are vital to the development of inclusive education. Collaborative learning is more than just something that technology might make easier. Collaboration is as basic to us as the air we breathe (Collins *et al.*, 2002). By learning from each other, we can begin to build inclusion.

> I think differences make the world go round, kids need to know that.
>
> *(Kate, London, quoted in Burke and Grosvenor, 2003, p. 103)*

References

Bainbridge, W. S., Burger, R., Canton, J., Golledge, R., Horn, R. E., Kuekes, P., Loomis, J., Murray, C. A., Penz, P., Pierce, B. M., Pollack, J., Robinett, W., Spohrer, J., Turkle, S. and Wilson, L. T. (2002) 'Expanding human cognition and communication: Theme B summary' in Roco, M. C. and Bainbridge, W. S. (eds) (2002) *Converging Technologies for Improving Human Performance: Nanotechnology, Biotechnology, Information Science and Cognitive Science*, Arlington, VA, National Science Foundation.

Batterson, J. G. and Pope, A. T. (2002) 'Converging technologies: a K-12 education vision' in Roco, M. C. and Bainbridge, W. S. (eds) (2002) *Converging Technologies for Improving Human Performance: Nanotechnology, Biotechnology, Information Science and Cognitive Science*, Arlington, VA, National Science Foundation.

BBC (2002) 'Couple "choose" to have deaf baby' and 'Deaf designer baby: the issues', Monday 8 April: http://www.bbc.new.co.uk/1/hi/health [accessed 5 December 2003].

Burke, C. and Grosvenor, I. (2003) *The School I'd Like: children and young people's reflections on an education for the 21st century*, London, Falmer Press.

Campbell, A. (2003) 'The next big thing – evolution': http://www.open2.net/nextbigthing/evolution/evolution.htm [accessed 11 June 2003].

Centre for Racial Equality (2003) 'Ethnic minorities in Britain: factsheet': http://www.cre.gov.uk/pdfs/em_fs.pdf [accessed 11 June 2003].

Collins, J., Harkin, J. and Nind, M. (2002) *Manifesto for Learning*, London, Continuum.

Culham, A. and Nind, M. (2003) 'A critical analysis of normalisation: clearing the way for inclusion', *Journal of Intellectual and Developmental Disability*, **28**(1), pp. 65–78.

Dautenhahn, K. and Werry, I. (2001) 'The AURORA Project: using mobile robots in autism therapy', online newsletter of IEEE Computer Society Learning Technology Task Force (LTTF), **3**(1), January: http://www.lttf.ieee.org [accessed 11 June 2003].

Dawkins, R. (1989). *The Selfish Gene*, Oxford, Oxford University Press.

Derbyshire, D. (2003) 'State must let parents judge, says DNA guru', *The Telegraph*: http://www.telegraph.co.uk/news/main [accessed 11 June 2003].

Department of Education and Science (DES) (1994) *Report of the Working Group on the Elimination of Sexism and Sex-stereotyping in Textbooks and Teaching Materials in Primary Schools*, An Roinn Oideachais, Baile Atha Cliath 1, the Republic of Ireland.

Down Syndrome: Health Issues (2003) CBS 48 Hours: 'Hype or hope?': http://www.ds-health.com/48hrs.htm [accessed 5 December 2003].

English Teachers Network (2003) 'Predictions – quotes': http://www.etni.org.il/quotes/future.htm [accessed 24 March 2002].

Gingrick, N. (2002) 'Vision for the converging technologies' in Roco, M. C. and Bainbridge, W. S. (eds) (2002) *Converging Technologies for Improving Human Performance: Nanotechnology, Biotechnology, Information Science and Cognitive Science*, Arlington, VA, National Science Foundation.

The Golden House-Sparrow Award (2001) 'Book of the week': http://www.hedweb.com/bokowfil.htm [accessed 11 June 2003].

The Guardian (2003) 25 July: http://society.guardian.co.uk/drugsandalcohol/html [accessed December 2003].

Hampshire County Council (2003) 'Wot's this about WAP and why?': http://www.hants.gov.uk/education/ngfl/subject/webtools/wap.html [accessed 11 June 2003].

Hurst, R. (2003) 'Conclusion: enabling or disabling globalisation' in Swain, J., French, S. and Cameron, C. (eds) *Controversial Issues in a Disabling Society*, Buckingham, Open University Press.

Hussain, Y., Atkin, K. and Ahmad, W. (2002) *South Asian Disabled Young People and their Families*, Bristol, The Policy Press.

International Centre for Bioethics, Culture and Disability (2003) 'Mission': http://www.bioethicsanddisability.org/start.html [accessed 11 June 2003].

Johnson, J. and Hirst, A. (2001) 'The Blue Peter RoboFesta robot design competition': http://robofesta.open.ac.uk/report2/ [accessed 11 June 2003].

Kearsley, G. (2000) *Online Education: learning and teaching in Cyberspace*, London, Thomson Learning.

Lipsy, D. K. and Gartner, A. (1997) *Inclusion and School Reform: transforming America's classrooms*, Baltimore, Paul H. Brookes.

Lister, I. (1975) *The School of the Future: some teachers' views on education in the year 2000*, London, Council for Educational Technology.

Mandela, N. (1995) *A Long Walk to Freedom*, London, Abacus.

McArthur, D., Lewis, M. W. and Bishay, M. (1993) 'The roles of artificial intelligence in education: current progress and future prospects': http://www.rand.org/education/mcarthur/papers/roleab.html [accessed 11 June 2003].

McGee, P., Day, T. and Sheehy, K. (2000) 'Evaluation of *Units of Sound*, a software programme for pupils with specific learning disabilities', commissioned research report submitted to the Department of Education and Science (DES) Republic of Ireland, July.

Monk, D. (2000) 'Theorising education law and childhood: constructing the ideal pupil', *British Journal of Sociology of Education*, **21**(3), pp. 355–70.

Murphy, E. (1996) '*Being Digital* by Nicholas Negroponte: Review': http://www.stemnet.nf.ca/~elmurphy/emurphy/digital.html [accessed 11 June 2003].

Murray, J. H. (1997) *Hamlet on the Holodeck: the future of narrative in cyberspace*, Cambridge, Mass., MIT Press.

New Internationalist (2002) 'Inside business corporate influence: the facts', NI347: http://www.newint.org/index4.html [accessed 11 June 2003].

Nind, M. and Hewett, D. (1994) *Access to Communication: developing the basics of communication with people with severe learning difficulties through intensive interaction*, London, David Fulton.

Nind, M. and Powell, S. (2000) 'Intensive interaction and autism: some theoretical concerns', *Children & Society*, **14**(2), pp. 98–109.

Oliver, M. (2001) 'Disability issues in the postmodern world' in Barton, L. (ed.) *Disability, Politics and the Struggle for Change*, London, David Fulton Publishers.

Papert, S. (1997a) 'Why school reform is impossible', *The Journal of the Learning Sciences*, **6**(4), pp. 417–27.

Papert, S. (1997b) 'Looking at technology through school-colored spectacles' http://www.papert.org/articles/ lookingattechnologythroughschool.html [accessed 4 April 2004].

Phespirit (2003) 'Momus – "Smart Drugs"' http://www.phespirit.info/ momus/19960107.htm [accessed 11 June 2003].

Reiser, R. (2001) 'The struggle for inclusion: the growth of a movement' in Barton, L. (ed.) *Disability, Politics and the Struggle For Change*, London, David Fulton Publishers.

Revell, P. (2003) 'Facing assault': http://education.guardian.co.uk/ [accessed 4 September 2003].

Ritchie, P. (2000) 'Why imagination matters': www.shstrust.org.uk/ downloads/imaginebetter.pdf (accessed 11 June 2003).

Rock, P. J. (1996) 'Eugenics and euthanasia: a cause for concern for disabled people, particularly disabled women', *Disability & Society*, **11**(1), pp. 121–27.

Roco, M. C. and Bainbridge, W. S. (eds) (2002) *Converging Technologies for Improving Human Performance: Nanotechnology, Biotechnology, Information Science and Cognitive Science*, Arlington, VA, National Science Foundation.

Selwyn, N. and Gorard, S. (2002) *The Information Age: technology, learning and exclusion in Wales*, Cardiff, University of Wales Press.

Spohrer, J. (2002) 'NBICS (NANO-BIO-INFO-COGNO-SOCIO) convergence to improve human performance: opportunities and challenges' in Roco, M. C. and Bainbridge, W. S. (eds) (2002) *Converging Technologies for Improving Human Performance: Nanotechnology, Biotechnology, Information Science and Cognitive Science*, Arlington, VA, National Science Foundation.

Stephenson, N. (2000) *The Diamond Age: or a young lady's illustrated primer*, London, Bantam Press.

Thomas, G. and Loxley, A. (2001) *Deconstructing Special Education and Constructing Inclusion*, Buckingham, Open University Press.

Universal Design Institute (2003): http://www.arch.umanitoba.ca/cibfd/about.htm [accessed 5 December 2003].

Wolbring, G. (2002) 'Science and technology and the triple D (Disease, Disability and Defect) vision' in Roco, M. C. and Bainbridge, W. S. (eds) (2002) *Converging Technologies for Improving Human Performance: Nanotechnology, Biotechnology, Information Science and Cognitive Science*, Arlington, VA, National Science Foundation.

Wolbring, G. (2003) 'Short biography', International Center for Bioethics, Culture and Disability: http://www.bioethicsanddisability.org/aboutme.html [accessed 11 June 2003].

Acknowledgements

Grateful acknowledgement is made to the following for permission to reproduce material in this book.

Unit 13

Tables

Table 13.1: Frost, R. (2001) 'Children and teachers with special needs' in Dadds, M. and Hart, S. (eds) *Doing Practitioner Research Differently*, p. 21, Taylor and Francis Books Ltd, www.tandf.co.uk and www.eBookstore.tandf.co.uk, many Taylor and Francis and Routledge books are now available in ebooks; *Table 13.2*: Thomas, G., Walker, D. and Webb, J. (1998) *The Making of the Inclusive School*, Taylor and Francis Books Ltd.

Unit 14

Figures

Figure 14.1: Wallace, M. and Pocklington, K. (2002), Figure 3.2: Responses to an externally initiated policy at the sites of implementation, in *Managing Complex Educational Change*, p. 67, Taylor and Francis Ltd; *Figure 14.2*: Hopkins, D. (2001) *School Improvement for Real*, Taylor and Francis Ltd; *Figure 14.3*: ICT as a tool for active learning – the learning cycle, based on a process model of learning (Kolb 1984; Dennison and Kirk 1990) from *Literacy Today*, December 2000, The National Literacy Trust. © Phil Taylor.

Illustrations

Page 57: © Steve Bell; *Pages 69, 71, 74 and 75*: Gary Rees.

Unit 15

Illustrations

Page 105: John Birdsall; *Page 106*: Sally and Richard Greenhill; *Page 107*: *Nottingham Evening Post*; *Page 123*: The Children's Society.

Unit 16

Illustrations

Pages 141 and 156: David Brown; *Pages 148, 149 and 150*: © The Open University; *Page 155*: Official photo from the International Snoezelen Association; *Pages 167 and 168*: Burke, C. and Grosvenor, I. (2003) *The School I'd Like*, RoutledgeFalmer.

Every effort has been made to contact copyright holders. If any have been inadvertently overlooked the publishers will be pleased to make the necessary arrangements at the first opportunity.